DEVELOPING

THE
DYNAMICS
OF
CORPORATE
GATHERING

BY FRANK DAMAZIO

DEVELOPING

THE
DYNAMICS
OF
CORPORATE
GATHERING

BY FRANK DAMAZIO

The Leadership Series • Volume 2

BIBLE TEMPLE
PUBLISHING
7545 N.E. Glisan St.
Portland, OR 97213
(503) 253-9020

Scripture quotations are taken from the
translations noted after each Scripture.

Note: In some Scripture quotations italics
have been added by the author
for emphasis.

Developing the Dynamics of Corporate Gathering

ISBN 0-914936-83-2

Printed in the United States of America

Foreword

Frank Damazio represents the restoration of the teacher gift to the body of Christ. Coupled with a godly personal life and a very successful church, Frank has a special anointing to dig out the truths in God's Word that will change your life and your church.

I recommend *Corporate Gatherings* as a "must read" book for you. Only as we begin to perceive in-depth the importance of our "particular" place in the body of Christ will we be able to walk in the fullness of the measure of the stature of Christ. Being "fitly joined together" is the secret to releasing God's power to you and through you.

Joyfully I discovered this secret not only in the pages of Pastor Damazio's writing but in functional reality in his life and ministry. Read this book carefully and prayerfully. It will change your life.

Abiding in Christ,

Dr. Larry Lea
Pastor, Church on the Rock

Dedication

I would like to dedicate this book to the church family of Eugene Christian Fellowship. You have made pastoring a joy, and meeting with you in our corporate gatherings has brought spiritual power into my life. May we as a church body always gather with great expectancy and clear purpose in mind.

Contents

Preface

The concept for this book has been in the birthing process for a long time. I have attended church for thirty years—
the last six as senior pastor of a vibrant, growing church. Over
the years the significance of public worship services has
become etched in my mind.

So many pressures and commitments consume people's
schedules today. Why should they make time to attend church?
What do we have to offer that would make them choose a
church service over another activity?

As leaders, we must spend more time in praying, plan-
ning, and coordinating simple but powerful congregational
meetings that attract people to the place where Jesus is
preached, spiritual growth occurs, and needs are met. To aid
you in this process this book is both theological and practical.
Along with biblical foundations for developing corporate services, you will find practical examples from the Old and New
Testaments. A consistent approach to applying these principles
by teaching, exhorting, and encouraging our congregations
will allow the biblical vision for powerful services to emerge.

Corporate gatherings are vital to the growth of every
Christian. Let us learn to make our services inspiring,
challenging, and exciting as we journey together to discover
the keys to dynamic corporate gatherings.

Pastor Frank Damazio

1

Corporate Gatherings: The Law of Degeneration

Left alone, everything in nature degenerates. Beautiful white carnations become wilted and brown. Growing children exhibit apathetic, insolent behavior. Neatly trimmed sheep lapse into scraggly herds. These sad consequences result from lack of care—the same care that spiritual "flocks" require.

In Acts 20:28, Paul exhorts the overseers to care for "all the flock." A flock speaks of all the sheep together as one body, the whole, but composed of individual sheep. Thus the object of the pastor's work is the flock, the whole body, as well as each member in particular. It is vital that the pastor continually and wisely discern the meeting of needs. In scriptural terms, he is a "watchman"; that is, he is to watch the overall flow of the church, the many different aspects and areas of the church that could degenerate or go astray without pastoral care and ministry. He is to ask himself: Why are some areas of the church, including corporate gatherings, doing well and some are not? Is the worship stagnant or exciting? Is the music orderly or disorderly? Is the overall attitude of the flock healthy or unhealthy?

To understand this more fully, we must realize there is a Law of Degeneration at work. This law is illustrated in the book of Jeremiah.

Jeremiah 2:21. Yet I had planted thee a noble vine, wholly a right seed: how then art thou turned into the degenerate plant of a strange vine unto me?

Thus there is a stage of growth in the local church where truths are planted. As time passes, the original planting can produce the "noble vine" that Jeremiah speaks of, or it can become a "strange vine." The plant will generate *or* degenerate.

As we teach truth and plant the right seed, much energy, emphasis, prayer, and teaching is used in this sowing process. Despite the cost, we must energetically maintain the truth or it will decay. A look at four different definitions of the word "degenerate" brings us a fuller meaning:

1. Hebrew = "to be removed from"

2. *Webster's Dictionary* = "having sunk below a former or normal condition or character, to deteriorate from a former standard"

3. Biology = "to become gradually of a lower type, a gradual falling off to a lower form of development"

4. Medicine = "change in health of the vital organs by injury or disease and leading to a loss of vitality, loss of proper function"

All these definitions can be related to our corporate gatherings. The degeneration is not sudden. Instead, there is a *gradual loss* of spiritual power in the body and worship services.

To ensure that this degeneration does not happen, overseers are given a two fold responsibility in Hebrews 13:17—"to watch and pray." Thus overseers are responsible to "watch and pray" in regard to the corporate gatherings or church services. Sometimes we approach this area with an underlying belief that corporate gatherings are self-adjusting and self-improving. This, of course, is not true. Corporate gatherings may degenerate as quickly as any other area without proper pastoral attention. We need to examine ourselves and the church services by asking some subtly complex questions:

• Are we satisfied with the spiritual quality of our public gatherings?

2

- Are we accomplishing our short-range and long-range benefits for the people?
- Are we diluting our corporate gatherings with things that do not edify the flock or help the service?
- Are we approaching our corporate gatherings with prayerfulness, as well as definite goals and purposes?
- Are we following any traditions and procedures that have little or no biblical base and, in fact, are hindering a fresh flow of the Holy Spirit?
- Are we in a spiritual rut that is causing stagnation and death?

There can be *multiple* causes for *one* result. We as pastors and leaders are all striving for biblical results in our corporate gatherings. Many churches meet together three or four times a week—twice on Sunday, a midweek service, and a prayer meeting, for example. The pastoral overseers are responsible to make these times profitable and challenging. Thus leaders must develop skills and abilities to create vitality in corporate gatherings and discern biblical strategies to maintain a spiritually healthy congregational meeting.

Some churches have cut back on the general assembly due to lack of support from the members, low attendance, negative comments, or just a basic no-interest attitude. The pastor should not turn a deaf ear to these remarks and attitudes; rather, he should respond with a biblical solution, such as one discussed later in this book, not a human reaction. Increasing numbers of churches are retreating to one main gathering a week, not because of biblical mandate, but because of lack of support from the congregation. Other churches have decided to use special events to boost the attendance on Sunday nights and at midweek services with films, skits, plays, singing groups, and so forth, but what are the long-term, spiritual benefits of such gatherings? I will discuss this issue more in Chapter 4.

I believe the Bible is very clear in establishing the importance of corporate gatherings. These times were meant to impart spiritual health and strength to our members. This demands a concerted effort on our parts as leaders and a clear understanding of what the Bible says about developing corporate gatherings and the threats to this effort. A personal experience will help to illustrate this chapter.

Several years ago I was asked to minister at one of the great churches of our nation. It had in years past been a large church with a great missionary vision that resulted in touching nations for the Lord. I was excited and eager to be exposed to such a great church. The surprise was both painful and instructional to me as a pastor. The church had dropped in attendance to just a handful, the congregation probably averaged in age of those present about 60 years of age. There were no youth. There were no young couples. There was no excitement. The Glory had departed and they didn't even know it. It was *pitiful*. It was *tragic*. It was a *tremendous lesson*. The church services will not always be dynamic and resulting in both numerical and spiritual growth if the leadership does not successfully build for a dynamic church. Corporate gathering of God's people is meant to be life changing, exciting, forever in transition. Let us beware of the degeneration process that is crouching at all our church doors.

2

Corporate Gatherings: The Spirit of Our Day

In our day it is evident that two spirits are at work—the Holy Spirit and the satanic spirit. An insidious manifestation of the latter is the spirit of humanism. As humanistic thinking festers in the lives of our people, it results in the "spirit of alienation" and the "spirit of Cain." Humanism is quite destructive to spiritual growth and healthy body life. In this Chapter, I will examine these three satanic spirits—humanism, alienation, and Cain—how people are snared in them, and how to use spiritual weapons to combat them.

Spirit #1: Spirit of Humanism

Many times in our corporate gatherings we feel the strong sense of the Holy Spirit's moving among us. Yet an undercurrent of doubt or skepticism may also be felt. This second presence is often traceable to the spirit of humanism, which affects our members much more than we realize. They are bombarded with self-oriented, humanistic messages on every side—in advertising of all types, on television shows, in newspapers and books, in schools at every age level, and from the attitudes of their peers, as well as society's leaders. The creeping effect on Christians is so subtle that we often do not discern that it is even happening, let alone presents a problem—until their foundations are eroded and their lives in turmoil.

What is humanism? In essence, humanism elevates self above God. A quote from the *Humanist Manifesto* (1933) is revealing:

We consider the religious forms and ideas of our

fathers no longer adequate. The quest for the good life is still the central task for mankind. Man is at last becoming aware that *he* alone is responsible for the realization of the world of his dreams, that *he* has within *himself* the power for its achievements. *He* must set intelligence and will to the task.[1] *(Italics mine.)*

The spirit of today's society, in which man considers himself to be above all things, is actually ruled from the spiritual kingdom. This scripture from Ephesians sheds light on this relationship.

Ephesians 2:2. Wherein time past ye walked according to the course of this world, according to the prince of the power of the air, the spirit that now worketh in the children of disobedience.

Before we became Christians, we walked after the spirit of the world. We were influenced by the spirit of the air who is, of course, Satan himself, whose fallen spirit molds the people of our day in his image. The following verses speak expressly of Satan's problem with self.

Isaiah 14:12-15. How art thou fallen from heaven, O Lucifer, son of the morning! how art thou cut down to the ground,which didst weaken the nations!

For thou hast said in thine heart, *I will* ascend into heaven, *I will* exalt my throne above the stars of God: *I will* sit also upon the mount of the congregation in the sides of the north:

I will ascend above the heights of the clouds; *I will* be like the most High.

Yet thou shalt be brought down to hell, to the sides of the pit.

Satan says "I will" five times in this short passage. It is the same "I will" we hear spoken so many times today by a society that believes self is higher than God, that there is no

6

God who is omnipresent, omniscient, and omnipotent. Satan's nature is expressed in the spirit of humanism:

1. The spirit of self-will
2. The spirit of independency
3. The problem with ego, self

All these areas blend into a philosophy that can be summed up in two statements: "I don't need God," and "I don't need anybody." Humanists believe prayer to God is unproven, outmoded faith. Salvationism is harmful, diverting people with false hope, (*Humanist Manifesto II*, 1973)[2]. Thus as Satan's nature is threefold, so the spirit of humanism in our day also breaks down into three areas:

1. *The spirit of selfishness:* The desire to please, serve and live for oneself. This problem of self-interest is the spirit of Lucifer's rising up to get what he wanted.

2. *The spirit of independency:* The desire to be one's own master without any accoutability to anyone, to answer only to self. Satan's goal was to usurp God's authority and to rule all of creation, including man.

3. *The spirit of solitariness:* The desire to live for oneself, to isolate one's actions and energies from the community of God, as Satan did. Problems such as isolated, apathetic individuals and fragmented families often result. Families and individuals relocate frequently, detaching themselves out of restlessness and lack of roots. This mobility brings a sense of detachment from their neighborhood, city, church, extended family—everyone but his or her own private existence. This same restlessness is seen in church-hopping where people change church families without biblical mandate or Holy Spirit guidance.

Spirit #2: Spirit of Alienation

Alienation results when the spirit of humanism enters the life of the Christian. Instead of being a fruitful, joyful member of the body of Christ, a person becomes a loner, isolated from

7

the needs of others and uninvolved. The Bible speaks of this in Ephesians 4:18 as "being alienated from the life of God." Alienation can take place before salvation because of sin, or after salvation because of our wrong attitudes that cause us to be isolated from the life flow in the body.

The New Testament word for alienation is defined: "to be estranged; to shut oneself out from the fellowship and intimacy; to withdraw your heart, affections; to be a non-participant; to live as an outsider." Obviously, this type of attitude hinders growth. A Christian in such a state is:

1. Saved, but alienated, withdrawn.
2. Saved, but maintaining an independent attitude and lifestyle.
3. Saved, but not maturing in corporate growth.
4. Saved, but remaining under the former spirit.

He is alienated from true Christianity and from the abundant life God intended him to enjoy as part of the body of Christ.

One major cause of alienation is unresolved offenses or conflicts. The Bible speaks of this as a sign of the times.

Matthew 24:10. (AMP) And then many will be *offended* and repelled and begin to *distrust* and *desert* (Him Whom they ought to trust and obey) and will stumble and fall away, and betray one another and pursue one another with hatred.

The New Testament word "offense" comes from the Greek in two forms: *skandalizo*, which is used 30 times in the New Testament, and *skandalon*, which is used 15 times. The root word here has the meaning "to spring forward and back, to slam shut"; the means whereby "one is closed in or trapped without escape." In hunting this would be called a "bait-stick," on which meat or some kind of lure would be attached to entice the prey to take the bait and become trapped. In human terms, "offense" is defined in the following ways:

8

1. An obstacle on the path over which one falls, is stumbl-
ed or hindered;
2. The cause of moral or spiritual ruin;
3. To suffer injury, to come to hurt;
4. To cause a person to begin to distrust and desert one
whom he ought to trust and obey, to be hindered from
acknowledging his authority.

Unresolved offenses lead to strained relationships; distrust;
isolation; harassment from the Enemy; emotional instability;
hindrances to the flow of the Holy Spirit; resentment; bitter-
ness; and betrayal. Any one of these attitudes, if left unchecked,
will damage the unit of the body of Christ and cause public
gatherings to be something less than what God intended them
to be.

Spirit #3: Spirit of Cain

We must also continually combat the attitudes of
selfishness which can easily be seen in the words of Cain.

Genesis 4:9. (LIVING) But afterwards the Lord asked Cain, "Where
is your brother? Where is Abel?"

"How should I know?" Cain retorted. "Am I supposed to keep track
of him wherever he goes?"

Cain's selfish spirit is satanic, greatly hindering true caring in the church. The Hebrew word used in Genesis 4:9,
translated "keeper," is the word *raah*, which means "to
shepherd, tend, look upon with pleasure, to hedge about so
as to guard or to protect." Cain was supposed to feel strongly
protective about his brother. He was supposed to shepherd
Abel; instead Cain allowed selfish ambition to cloud his
thoughts and pervert his motives.

Jude 11 cautions us against taking on this destructive attitude: "Woe unto them, for they have gone the *way of Cain*."
Many have gone the "way of Cain" today. They feel no respon-

9

sibility to other people; they have no heart for really protecting their brother or sister in Christ from harm. In I John 3:11-17, we learn that Cain was of the Wicked One, the Devil. The Enemy utilizes the spirit of Cain to destroy all covenant relationships in the body of Christ.

To sum up, Satan is the "prince of the power of the air" who rules over and promotes humanism, the spirit of alienation, and the spirit of Cain. We who have been redeemed are liberated from this independent life. The Cross of Calvary brought a contrasting attitude to the new man—that of togetherness, accountability, and caring. These opposing philosophies are graphically portrayed in the following chart where the "old man" is ruled by self, the "new man" by the Holy Spirit.

"Time Past"	"But Now"
Ephesians 2:1-3	Ephesians 2:13-22

Spirit of the Enemy	*Spirit of Christ*
• Self-will	• God's will
• Self-interest	• Body-interest
• Self-desiring	• Body-desiring
• Self-pleasing	• Body-pleasing
• Self-governing	• Body-governing

Independent	• Quickened together	(Ephesians 2:5)
Selfish	• Raised together	(Ephesians 2:6)
Solitary	• Seated together	(Ephesians 2:6)
Humanistic	• United as family	(Ephesians 2:19)
	• Framed together	(Ephesians 2:21)
	• Builded together	(Ephesians 2:22)
	• Joined together	(Ephesians 4:16)
	• Assembling together	(Hebrews 10:25)

The key words from either side of this chart are "self" and "together." We have been redeemed from the spirit of self that destroys the spirit of togetherness. The Bible describes this togetherness as "covenant community." The church in Acts aptly portrays what it means to be brought together in covenant community.

Acts 1:14. . .continued in one accord. . .

Acts 2:1. . .they were all with one accord in one place. . .

Acts 2:41. . .they were added unto them. . .

Acts 2:44. . .all that believed were together. . .

Acts 2:46. . .And they, continuing daily with one accord in the temple, and breaking bread from house to house, did eat their meat with gladness and singleness of heart.

Webster's Dictionary defines community as "a society of people having common rights and privileges, common interests, living under the same laws and regulations, having a community spirit."

The biblical concept, "covenant community," is depicted in the following statements:

1. Covenant community exists when people are more concerned with the corporate local body than with themselves. Corporate life becomes more important than the individual's own pleasure or will.

2. Covenant community exists when individuals are being knitted, builded, framed, and joined together. This speaks of close, long-lasting, real friendships.

3. Covenant community exists when the spirit of sacrifice becomes the attitude in which the community meets the needs of all.

4. Covenant community exists when people want to spend time together in both spiritual and natural activities: church services, picnics, camps, home meetings, sports, family

activities, such as baby showers, and so forth.

5. Covenant community exists when the elderly retain proper godly authority throughout their lives and are cherished and respected by the community.

6. Covenant community exists when the family is in biblical order: the husband or father taking his rightful place as head of the home; the wife finding fulfillment in this atmosphere; the children being well-disciplined, happy, and secure.

7. Covenant community exists when humanism, selfishness, independence, and isolation are treated as intruding viruses. They are overcome and destroyed by applying the Word of God so that covenant community may become a reality.

How can the local church combat the spirits of humanism, alienation, and Cain to enjoy vital, spiritually-refreshing corporate gatherings? The answer lies in cultivating covenant community attitudes. A study of Romans 14:1-15:5 details seven vital attitudes for successful community living which precede successful corporate gatherings.

1. The attitude of acceptance and understanding of each other.

Romans 14:1-6. (NKJV) Receive one who is weak in the faith, but not to disputes over doubtful things.

For one believes he may eat all things, but he who is weak eats only vegetables.

Let not him who eats despise him who does not eat, and let not him who does not eat judge him who eats; for God has received him.

Who are you to judge another's servant? To his own master he stands or falls. Indeed, he will be made to stand, for God is able to make him stand.

One person esteems one day above another; another esteems every day alike. Let each be fully convinced in his own mind.

He who observes the day, observes it to the Lord; and he who does not observe the day, to the Lord he does not observe it. He who eats, eats to the Lord, for he gives God thanks; and he who does not eat, to the Lord he does not eat, and gives God thanks.

The strong shall receive the weak without judgement. We need to give each other room to fail, to be different. We also need to guard against jealousy, anger, and envy. Our sole concern should be to edify and encourage one another to maturity in Christ, minus our ego gratification at the expense of others.

2. The attitude of accountability to each other.

Romans 14:7. (NKJV) For none of us lives to himself, and no one dies to himself.

We must realize that no man lives solely to himself. No selfish conduct edifies. Instead, every action—and the motivation behind that action—is ultimately felt by the people around us. We also must realize that accountability is not optional. Hebrews 3:13 commands us to "exhort one another daily" to be accountable. Without this attitude, sin will prevail, and weak families, weak churches, and weak nations will result.

3. The attitude of responsibility concerning each other's walk.

Romans 14:13. (NKJV) Therefore let us not judge one another anymore, but rather resolve this, not to put a stumbling block or a cause to fall in our brother's way.

We must identify with the feelings of others and seek to gently but firmly restore them when necessary. As Galatians 6:1 describes, we are not to be stumbling blocks. In the Greek, "stumbling block" is defined as "something set in a man's path to trip him up; a cause of falling; a snare; a bait; a lure; to entice astray so as to ruin." Our attitudes—and the words and actions that proceed from them—can be either constructive or destructive. We can be the type of people who restore others and encourage them on in their walks, or who tear them down through criticism, gossip, pride, and envy. We can provide others with a sense of refuge or a sense of insecurity.

4. The attitude of sensitivity to our brother's weaknesses.

Romans 14:15, 17. (NKJV) Yet if your *brother* is *grieved* because of your food, you are no longer walking in *love.* Do not destroy with your food the one for whom Christ died.

For the kingdom of God is not food and drink, but righteousness and peace and joy in the Holy Spirit.

Verse 15 states the principle by which we have titled this point. This scripture clearly states that we as Christians can hurt one another by careless actions that seem to be harmless. The real issue here is not necessarily eating but *personal rights* and *freedoms.* If something we do causes a brother to be hurt, then we are clearly not walking in love but in selfishness and insensitivity.

For the sake of clarity, consider my paraphrase of verse 17: "For the kingdom of God is not holding on to personal rights and freedoms, but serving your brother in love, which results in righteousness, joy, and peaceful relationships."

This passage reminds us that we must not let our liberty be a stumbling block or snare to anyone else. First Corinthians 8:9-12 instructs us that when we weaken our brother, we are sinning against him and also sinning against Christ. Paul gives us a solution in verse 13: "Wherefore, if meat *(or any personal freedom)* make my brother to offend, I will eat no flesh *(or carry out no particular personal freedom)* while the world standeth, lest I make my brother to offend."

5. The attitude of edification that brings a bond of peace.

14

> **Romans 14:19.** (NKJV) Therefore let us pursue the things which make for peace and the things by which one may edify another.

We are not to have the attitude of selfish ambition as noted in Philippians 2:3, because it destroys edification. Instead, we are to follow the principle given in verse 4: "Look not every man on his own things, but every man also on the things of others." We are to be considerate of one another's needs, shortcomings, hurts and joys, responding to those areas with true love and concern. This love replaces the worldly facade of pretending to care while simply waiting for the opportunity to pour out our own problems.

6. The attitude of not being a self-pleaser.

> **Romans 15:1-3.** (NKJV) We then who are strong ought to bear with the scruples of the weak and not to please ourselves.
> Let each of us please his neighbor for his good, leading to edification.
> For even Christ did not please Himself; but as it is written, "The reproaches of those who reproached You fell on Me."

This scriptural principle is aptly described in the scripture given with this point. Paul echoes this theme in I Corinthians 10:33, "Even as I please men in all things, not seeking mine own profit, but the profit of many, that they may be saved." Seeking the needs of others provides that everyone's needs are met, thus guaranteeing healthy body life, as well as healthy corporate gatherings.

7. The attitude of identification with one another's problems—past or present.

> **Romans 15:4-7.** (NKJV) For whatever things were written before were written for our learning, that we through the patience and comfort of the Scriptures might have hope.

Now may the God of patience and comfort grant you to be like-minded toward one another, according to Christ Jesus.

That you may with one mind and one mouth glorify the God and Father of our Lord Jesus Christ.

Therefore receive one another, just as Christ also received us, to the glory of God.

We are to strive for the same kind of compassion that Christ demonstrated. He identified so totally with the needs, failures, and hopes of mankind that He was willing to die to redeem us, to take our sin upon Himself. In a lesser form, we can demonstrate compassion by praying for each other and by laying down our lives for one another. Paul exemplifies this principle in the Book of Philemon. He writes in verse 18, "If he hath wronged thee, or oweth thee ought (anything), put that on mine account." We must be willing to bear each other up as we grow in God, seeking each other's welfare before our own. In this way, humanism and its "prince," Satan, are defeated, and God is exalted in the rejoicing fellowship of believers.

3

Corporate Gatherings: The Biblical Perspective

In this chapter I wish to lay out a firm biblical base for corporate gatherings. This important truth will be proven and illustrated by these aids:

- A Hebrew definition of the word "assemble, assembly."
- Four illustrations from the Old Testament of corporate gatherings with obvious results.
- Three examples from the New Testament of the consequences of public meetings.

Definition

The Hebrew definition of the word "assemble" is particularly descriptive for our purposes. It means all of the following:

1. to grasp;
2. to collect together;
3. to scrape together;
4. to go forth and assemble as a man of war;
5. to assemble against the enemy;
6. a convocation together for a sacred thing;
7. a gathering together in one place;
8. to meet with anyone at an appointed place;
9. to come together for a specific purpose at a specific time and place (like being subpoenaed for court, a definite appointed meeting together with the other party).

From this rather lengthy definition we see that our corporate gatherings are not just casual meetings that God considers optional. He has made an appointment with us. Our response should be to sanctify this time, to set it aside specifically to meet with Him as a body. The following scriptures will enhance your personal study of the principle of assembling together. You will be amazed to see how God's power is displayed through the unity of His people.

Exodus 38:8	Psalm 89:7
Leviticus 8:4	Psalm 107:32
Leviticus 23:36	Psalm 111:1
Numbers 1:18	Proverbs 5:14
Numbers 8:9	Isaiah 4:5
Numbers 10:2-3	Isaiah 43:9
Numbers 20:6-8	Isaiah 45:20
Joshua 18:1	Joel 2:6, 3:1
I Samuel 2:22	Acts 1:4, 4:31
II Samuel 20:4-5	Acts 11:26, 15:25
II Chronicles 5:6	

Old Testament Illustrations

The Old Testament illustrates this concept of assembly and the power of congregational gatherings. Let's look at four examples.

Old Testament #1: Tabernacle of Moses

The first illustration is found in Exodus 24:8-9 and 40:3-5. As a type, the tabernacle of Moses demonstrates *covenant with God* through the priests and through the corporate gathering of the people in the presence of the Lord. The holy ceremony that God ordained for cleansing the priests at the laver and at the altar signify the purifying of our hearts, which is a prerequisite to entering God's presence individually or corporately. Verse 34 of Chapter 40 expresses powerfully what happens when God's Word is obeyed in the cleansing of our hearts. "Then a cloud covered the tent of the congregation, and the glory of the Lord filled the tabernacle." The New Testament parallel is the glory of God filling our houses of worship, which includes physical buildings as well as our physical bodies that have become "temples of the living God."

Old Testament #2: The Temple of Solomon

Our second illustration takes us to II Chronicles. Here we see the elaborate dedication of Solomon's temple. The final two verses paint a beautiful picture of the *power of unified worship* in corporate gatherings.

II Chronicles 5:11-14. It came even to pass, as the trumpeters and singers were as one, to make one sound to be heard in praising and thanking the Lord; and when they lifted up their voice with the trumpets and cymbals and instruments of music, and praised the Lord, saying, For he is good; for his mercy endureth for ever; that then the house was filled with a cloud, even the house of the Lord;

So that the priests could not stand to minister by reason of the cloud: for the glory of the Lord had filled the house of God.

Unified worship brings the "felt" power of God to our church services, allowing the Holy Spirit to move freely within hearts and lives. This release of the Spirit often results in souls saved, marriages healed, lives rededicated, ministries called, and so forth, as our people obey the inner promptings of the Lord.

Old Testament #3: The Restoration from Babylon

Ezra 10:1 provides the third illustration. This scripture denotes the *power of confession* and *cleansing in corporate gatherings*.

Ezra 10:1. Now when Ezra had prayed, and when he had confessed, weeping and casting himself down before the house of God, there assembled unto him out of Israel a very great congregation of women and children: for the people wept very sore.

19

Of special importance in this scripture is that Ezra—as the leader—set the example of confession for the people. He identified with their sin, just as Jesus did with ours, and paved the way for a release of God's power to forgive the people. Ezra's surrogate confession set a divine appointment for the Jews to again meet with God in covenant relationship.

Old Testament #4: The Restoration of Jerusalem

The fourth and final Old Testament illustration of congregational gathering is in Nehemiah 8:1. The wall of Jerusalem was rebuilt after some of the Jews returned from their exile in Babylon. The jews assembled in the seventh month. At peace with their enemies, they desired to hear from God. Verse 1 states, "And all the people gathered themselves together as one man into the street that was before the water gate; and they spake unto Ezra the scribe to bring the book of the law of Moses, which the Lord had commanded to Israel." The assembly was again a unified event: *the covenant of the law was renewed.*

Reading God's Word in corporate gatherings and instructing the congregation in its application brings repentance, restoration, and recommitment to walking in God's precepts (Nehemiah 10:28-29). This is God's principle of sowing and reaping which operates equally well in today's corporate gatherings.

New Testament Illustrations

The New Testament, as well, is rich in illustrations of assemblies or corporate gatherings. Let's look at three of them.

New Testament #1: The Church at Corinth

The Corinthian church is the subject of Paul's numerous discourses on proper corporate gatherings, making it an excellent illustration for our purposes. In this first letter to the Corinthians, Paul speaks of the power of the Lord Jesus Christ that is with them when they gather together.

I Corinthians 5:4. In the name of our Lord Jesus Christ, when ye are gathered together and my spirit, with the power of the Lord Jesus Christ, . . .

I Corinthians 11:20, 33. When ye come together therefore into one place, this is not to eat the Lord's supper.

Wherefore, my brethren, when ye come together to eat, tarry one for another.

Chapter 11, verses 20 and 33, refer to the Lord's Supper and some correction the Corinthians needed at this gathering.

Chapter 14 also gives two excellent examples of proper order when using the gifts of the Spirit in corporate gatherings.

I Corinthians 14:23. If therefore the whole church be come together into one place, and all speak with tongues, and there come in those that are unlearned, or unbelievers, will they not say that ye are mad?

I Corinthians 14:26. How is it then, brethren? when ye come together, every one of you hath a psalm, hath a doctrine, hath a tongue, hath a revelation, hath an interpretation. Let all things be done unto edifying.

New Testament #2: The Church of Jerusalem

Our second example comes from the Jerusalem church in the Book of Acts. Consistently applied principles of corporate gatherings were partly responsible for the vibrant power of the Holy Spirit in this church. In Acts 2:44 we see them as believers having all things in common. Everyone's physical, social, and spiritual needs are met. They gathered together regularly in communion, fellowship, teaching, and meals. Acts 4:31 describes the move of God as the church gathered together to pray.

Acts 4:31. And when they prayed, the place was shaken when they were assembled together; and they were all filled with the Holy Ghost, and they spake the word of God with boldness.

New Testament #3: The Church of Hebrew Believers

The Book of Hebrews provides our third and final illustration for corporate gatherings. In the following verses the writer warns of dire consequences resulting from a lack of attention and fervor for the spiritual training ground of God which exists when the people of God assemble.

Hebrews 10:24-25. And let us consider one another to provoke unto love and to good works:

Not forsaking the assembling of ourselves together, as the manner of some is; but exhorting one another: and so much the more, as ye see the day approaching.

The implication here is that those who neglect corporate gatherings eventually become isolated from the Spirit's movement in the local church. After a prolonged period of time, this condition often results in backsliding. Church attendance can be an accurate barometer of spiritual health where high readings indicate energy, health, and motivation for God . . . and low readings point to trouble brewing for the individual.

4

Corporate Gatherings: The Purpose

Just as the physical body requires certain elements such as vitamins and minerals for growth and health, so the church body has spiritual requirements. In terms of church assembly, Scripture gives us eight guiding and essential elements for gathering together. Each offers a vital function necessary to the spiritual growth and health of the church body.

Element #1. A fresh, challenging Word through God's ordained servants.

Romans 8:9-10. But ye are not in the flesh, but in the Spirit, if so be that the Spirit of God dwell in you. Now if any man have not the Spirit of Christ , he is none of His.

And if Christ be in you, the body is dead because of sin, but the Spirit is life because of righteousness.

Preaching in a corporate gathering must be more than a passing thought or a good exhortation. The Word must be preached like a two-edged sword cutting away hardness of heart, stubbornness of will, selfishness of life, and compromised faith. The Word must challenge people right where they are to advance in God. Too many leaders are preaching a diluted, social, "make-you-feel-good" message. Our generation needs to be challenged with a straightforward, biblical word. If corporate gatherings do not have this element of challenge, where will the people receive it?

Element #2. The Holy Spirit moving in the individual's body, mind, and Spirit convicting, changing, refreshing, and renewing.

Romans 12:1-2. I beseech you therefore, brethren, by the mercies of God, that ye present your bodies a living sacrifice, holy, acceptable unto God, which is your reasonable service.

And be not conformed to this world: but be ye transformed by the renewing of your mind, that ye may prove what is that good, acceptable, and perfect, will of God.

The Hebrew word for "renewal" is *hayah* which means "to be quickened; to recover health and strength; to refresh a person who is weary; to receive a new flow of spiritual life." When our people are showing signs of not enjoying the spiritual life-flow any longer, of losing interest in spiritual things, or of leaving their total surrender and first-love relationship, they are in need of renewal. Corporate gatherings provide a setting for conviction, repentance, and a fresh flow to begin again in their lives. Our ministry as leaders should be to provide the encouragement and motivation to renew the people's strength in the Lord (Isaiah 40:30-41; Luke 22:32); to renew their "altar" or heart to seek the Lord (II Chronicles 15:8, 12); to renew their spiritual warfare (Job 29:20); to renew their thinking (Ephesians 4:23); and to renew their inward man (II Corinthians 4:6).

Element #3. The proper use of spiritual gifts to strengthen, encourage, and build up each believer in the many-membered body of Christ.

I Corinthians 12:4, 7. Now there are diversities of gifts, but the same Spirit.

But the manifestation of the Spirit is given to every man to profit withal.

The powerful moving of the Holy Spirit during corporate gatherings provides a natural setting for the fruitful sharing of spiritual gifts. While this is not the only time these gifts can and should be manifested, unity of worship provides a channel for the Holy Spirit to flow easily. Order and harmony should characterize these times of encouragement to move in prophecy, song of the Lord, and Word of the Lord.

Calling a church a "body" does not make it so unless the members are effectively connected and joined together. Ministering the gifts of the Spirit to one another does just that.

Element #4. The framework for making important decisions.

I Corinthians 12:1-10. Now concerning spiritual gifts, brethren, I would not have you ignorant.

Ye know that ye were Gentiles, carried away unto these dumb idols, even as ye were led.

Wherefore I give you to understand, that no man speaking by the Spirit of God calleth Jesus accursed: and that no man can say that Jesus is the Lord, but by the Holy Ghost.

Now there are diversities of gifts, but the same Spirit.

And there are differences of administrations, but the same Lord.

And there are diversities of operations, but it is the same God which worketh all in all.

But the manifestation of the Spirit is given to every man to profit withal.

For to one is given by the Spirit the word of wisdom, to another the word of knowledge by the same Spirit;

To another faith by the same Spirit; to another the gifts of healing by the same Spirit;

To another the working of miracles; to another prophecy, to another discerning of spirits; to another divers kinds of tongues; to another the interpretation of tongues:

Although some decisions are finalized within the bounds of an elders' meeting, we must have a unified vision if our local church bodies are to go forward in strength, power, and enthusiasn. When a decision must be made, fervent worship, a refreshing and renewing of God's Word, and the operation of spiritual gifts set a tremendous atmosphere for all the people to hear from the Lord. Days of prayer and fasting before certain meetings are especially helpful when a concensus must be reached that is "peaceful and easy to be entreated" (James 3:17). This same principle applies on a personal level. People are continually faced with decisions concerning important areas of life. Corporate gatherings often supply answers through the ministry of the Holy Spirit and the Word.

Element #5. The significant corporate expression of the church in every given locality for the purpose of influencing the community for righteousness.

Matthew 28:18-20. And Jesus came and spake unto them, saying, All power is given unto me in heaven and in earth.

Go ye therefore, and teach all nations, baptizing them in the name of the Father, and of the Son, and of the Holy Ghost:

Teaching them to observe all things whatsoever I have commanded you; and, lo, I am with you alway, even unto the end of the world. Amen.

As we gather in the Spirit of the Lord, we express the love, unity, and power of God which draw us unto Him. We then dispense this message to the world as ambassadors, influencing our homes, our neighborhoods, our jobs, and our day-to-day lives, as well as our services when visitors or unbelievers are present.

Element #6. The reputation as an accessible place of refuge for all who seek help and encouragement.

Isaiah 4:1-6. And in that day seven women shall take hold of one man, saying, We will eat our own bread, and wear our own apparel: only let us be called by thy name, to take away our reproach.

In that day shall the branch of the Lord be beautiful and glorious, and the fruit of the earth shall be excellent and comely for them that are escaped of Israel.

And it shall come to pass, that he that is left in Zion, and he that remaineth in Jerusalem, shall be called holy, even every one that is written among the living in Jerusalem:

When the Lord shall have washed away the filth of the daughters of Zion, and shall have purged the blood of Jerusalem from the midst thereof by the spirit of judgment, and by the spirit of burning.

And the Lord will create upon ever dwelling place of Mount Zion, and upon her assemblies, a cloud and smoke by day, and the shining of a flaming fire by night: for upon all the glory shall be a defence.

And there shall be a tabernacle for a shadow in the daytime from the heat, and for a place of refuge, and for a cover from storm and from rain.

The Book of Zephaniah provides insight into the concept of corporate gatherings as a place of refuge. The name "Zephaniah" itself means "Jehovah hides, hidden of Jehovah, Jehovah conceals or protects." In the context of this Old Testament book, Zephaniah's name was prophetic. God wanted to bring His people under His wings and protect them from the coming Day of Judgment and wrath. However, He could not hide the people unless they brought their lives into order. God wants to protect us today from the judgment of sin in our lives. The Book of Zephaniah gives nine conditions for entering into the refuge of God. As individual members practice these principles, the corporate gatherings will become a hiding place:

1. We are not to conceal mixture, or idolatry, in our lives.

Zephaniah 1:4-6. (NIV) I will stretch out my hand against Judah and against all who live in Jerusalem. I will cut off from this place every remnant of Baal, the names of the pagan and idolatrous priests—those who bow down on the housetops to worship the starry host, those who bow down and swear by the Lord and who also swear by Molech, those who turn back from following the Lord and neither seek the Lord nor inquire of Him.

---

2. We are to inquire of the Lord and not draw back from, or refuse, His counsel.

Zephaniah 1:6, 3:2. (NIV) Those who turn back from following the Lord and neither seek the Lord nor inquire of Him.

She obeys no one, she accepts no correction. She does not trust in the Lord, she does not draw near to her God.

---

3. We are not to become slothful and complacent.

Zephaniah 1:12. (NIV) At that time I will search Jerusalem with lamps and punish those who are complacent, who are like wine left on its dregs, who think, "The Lord will do nothing, either good or bad."

---

4. We are not to dwell carelessly, without vision or principles.

Zephaniah 2:15, 3:16. (NIV) This is the carefree city that lived in safety. She said to herself, "I am, and there is none beside me." What a ruin she has become, a lair for wild beasts! All who pass by her scoff and shake their fists.

On that day they will say to Jerusalem, "Do not fear, O Zion: do not let your hands hang limp."

---

5. We are to obey the authority of God and His anointed leaders.

Zephaniah 3:1-2. (NIV) Woe to the city of oppressors, rebellious and defiled! She obeys no one, she accepts no correction. She does not trust in the Lord, she does not draw near to her God.

---

6. We are to respond to correction and receive the correction the Holy Spirit sends from the leadership.

Zephaniah 3:2, 7. (NIV) She obeys no one, she accepts no correction. She does not trust in the Lord, she does not draw near to her God. I say to the city, "Surely you will fear me and accept correction!"

7. We are to trust in the Lord and not in our strength.

Zephaniah 3:2. (NIV) She obeys no one, she accepts no correction. She does not trust in the Lord, she does not draw near to her God.

8. We are to receive a pure language to call on the name of the Lord and to discipline our words.

Zephaniah 3:9 (NIV) Then will I purify the lips of the peoples, that all of them may call on the name of the Lord and serve him shoulder to shoulder.

9. We are to rejoice, shout, and sing in Zion.

Zephaniah 3:14, 17. (NIV) Sing, O Daughter of Zion; shout aloud, O Israel! Be glad and rejoice with all your heart, O Daughter of Jerusalem! The Lord your God is with you, He is mighty to save. He will take great delight in you, He will quiet you with His love, He will rejoice over you with singing.

Element #7: The revealing of hearts openly and humbly before the Lord.

Psalm 84:7. They go from strength to strength, every one of them in Zion *appeareth* before God.

God's command to Israel in the Old Testament reveals a pattern we can copy as New Testament believers. He commanded Israel to appear before God three times a year: during the first month at Passover, during the third month at Pentecost, and during the seventh month at the Feast of Tabernacles. These were times for the people to slow down and hear from God. The word "appear" means "to reveal oneself, to open up so as to be inspected." Its meaning can be seen in the act of flaying and inspecting a sacrificial animal which revealed the inward parts by removing the outer hide. This is what God wanted His people to do at these special times—open themselves up for inspection.

God commanded Israel to appear before the Lord for five purposes:
- Personal inspection (Psalm 139:9)
- Spiritual renewal (Isaiah 57:14-15)
- Rehearing the Word of the Lord (Nehemiah 8:1-12)
- Renewing of vows to God (Psalm 61)
- Spiritual enlargement (Exodux 34:24; Psalm 119:32)

The Bible also tells us how we can prepare to appear before the Lord. Each of these factors is vital to full readiness for hearing the Spirit of God:
- Prayer (Acts 13:1-4)
- Confession and cleansing (Psalm 139:1-2; I John 1:7-9)
- Discipline of the Word and waiting (Psalm 130:5-6)
- Faith and expectation (Hebrews 11:1)
- Open ears (Isaiah 50:4-5; Revelation 2:11, 17)

Element #8. The powerful presence of God brought about by corporate worship.

Matthew 18:20. For where two or three are gathered together in my name, there am I in the midst of them.

This is the final, and most important, element of corporate gatherings. The supernatural presence of God must be realized to change our perspective from the human to the divine. Although this presence is not necessarily manifested in miracles or healings, the church must be a place where we encounter the living God and where we receive what we need in order to live a victorious life. As the psalmist says, ". . . in thy presence is fulness of joy . . .'" (Psalm 16:11), and "The hills melted like wax at the presence of the Lord . . ." (Psalm 97:5).

We do not gather together to be entertained, but to rejoice in His presence. Thus you and I as leaders should understand the principles that release God's presence to His people and emphasize them in each gathering. The first of these two main principles is *pre-service prayer*, where the people seek the Lord earnestly for personal cleansing and for God to anoint the service. The second principle is *biblical worship*, where the unity of praise and worship releases God's presence to inhabit His godly people. When these principles are practiced, Jesus will be in the midst of that gathering, and joy will be released to the people.

5

Corporate Gatherings: Leadership Responsibility

In all corporate gatherings there must be a united effort between the leadership and the congregation. Both must carry out their due responsibility to promote a successful moving of the Holy Spirit. In this chapter I will survey leadership responsibility, and in Chapter 6 examine the congregation's role.

Paul gives us key insights to corporate gatherings in his First Epistle to the Corinthian Church, especially Chapter 14. That passage, along with other key scriptures, will be the basis for our conclusions. In these verses we find seven vital functions of the leadership at corporate gatherings:

1. Edification
2. Exhortation
3. Comfort
4. Revelation

5. Knowledge
6. Prophecy
7. Doctrine

Responsibility #1: Edification. *Oikodome.*

I Corinthians 14:3. (NKJV) But he who prophesies speaks edification and exhortation and comfort to men.

The authority, and thus the responsibility, to edify the local church is given to leaders by God and is noted in II Corinthians 10:8 and 13:10. Chapter 10, verse 8, puts it this way, "For though I should boast somewhat more of our authority, which the Lord hath given us for edification, and not for your destruction, I should not be ashamed, . . ."

"Edify," or "edifying," is the Greek word *oikodomeo,* a noun meaning "to build or strengthen, the process of building or putting together." Another form of *oikodome* means "an edifice or construction." *Webster's Dictionary* defines "edification" as a "building up, in a moral or religious sense; instruction, improvement and progress of the mind, in knowledge, morals, faith and holiness." In Ephesians 2:22 a strengthened form of this word is used, referring to the saints being built together for God's habitation or dwelling place.

In the biblical sense, edification is every communication of divine truth which strengthens faith and spiritual life. It includes all true Christian instruction often called doctrine. Thus, edification is accomplished by enlightenment which enables hearers to inwardly grasp divine truth.

For further study on our authority and responsibility as leaders to edify the body, see the following scriptures: I Corinthians 14:3-5, 12, 17, 26; Ephesians 4:12, 16, 29; I Timothy 1:4; and Acts 9:31.

All of the scriptures listed above contain one particularly strong exhortation to leaders in the church: Excel in edifying. As an example, we could use I Corinthians 14:12, ". . . seek that ye may excel to the edifying of the church." As leaders we are to excel at building up the saints in every church service. The days we are living in are stressful and discouraging to many people, including Christians. Numerous church members are going through difficult seasons of life. They are being shaken and stripped in a cleansing "autumn," or tested and prepared through a trying "winter." Possibly, they are in a "spring," where God's Word is being developed and fulfilled in their lives, or they're in a marvelously fruitful "summer," a time of harvest and spiritual contentment.

Whatever the state of our flock, when we come together as a church, a true spirit of edification is vital. People need to be strengthened continually, especially in church services. The message we preach, the comments we make, the illustrations we use, and the attitudes in which we preach all greatly influence the ministry of edification. Everyone of us desires to keep high standards of righteousness, prayer, and commitment, but we must never discourage the people by berating them for not measuring up. We must strengthen and build them up so that they will be able to fulfill the standard of God's Word.

Responsibility #2: Exhortation: *Paraklesis.*

I Corinthians 14:3. (NKJV) But he who prophesies speaks edification and exhortation and comfort to men.

Scriptural precept for the leader to be an exhorter of the flock of God is found in the following scriptures: I Corinthians 14:3; Romans 12:8; Hebrews 6:18; Hebrews 12:5; Hebrews 13:22; Acts 4:36; Romans 15:4-5; and II Corinthians 1:3-5.

Exhortation is the Greek word *paraklesis*, which means "to exert influence upon the will and decision of another with the object of guiding him into a generally accepted code of behavior or of entreating him to observe certain instructions; to encourage those under pressure; to call someone to your side for the purpose of strengthening."

In a military context, *paraklesis* is common for encouragement of soldiers, as in II Maccabees 15:11, which talks about putting confidence into the troops, strengthening the morale of the soldiers by *paraklesis* from the law and the prophets and by recollection of past battles. Rehearsing, or retelling, past victories brought tremendous encouragement to those soldiers.

Paraklesis is always used in the sense of "speaking good words" to others so as to encourage them, to cheer them, to enliven them, and to reassure them." *Paraklesis* also has

35

the idea of the worshiper "calling in God" to a circumstance or situation he or she cannot handle. It is interesting to note that *paraklesis* is closely related to *parakletos*—the word used by the Lord Jesus when referring to the Holy Spirit. This word means "one sent out to be alongside," as one who "consoles us in times of affliction and sorrow," and who "entreats us with a view to our conduct."

Because these words are related, *paraklesis* also carries the meaning of "consolation; to encourage and help the suffering, afflicted, dying, and those treated unjustly; to write a letter or make a personal visit to those who have suffered tragedy." During the first century, comforters invited those needing consolation to come for treatment in a kind of clinic. The orator Antiphon wrote a consolatory letter to the afflicted and also undertook to cure the sorrowing of their grief by oral statements of kindness and love. Music was also used, called "sweet solace for terrible vexations."

Paraklesis is a main ingredient of a successful corporate gathering, because we life in a time when there are many comfortless people. Some of them are going through such heavy problems that their souls are almost closed to receiving consolation, as in Psalms 68:20 and 76:2. The comfortlessness of people finds moving expression in Lamentations, especially 1:2, 9, 16, and 2:13. For example, verse 16 says, "For these things I weep; mine eye runneth down with water, because the comforter that should relieve my soul is far from me; my children are desolate, because the enemy prevailed." This desolation comes partly from God Himself as a judgment upon sin—today in history and tomorrow at the Last Judgment. Leaders must discern why some people will not be comforted and either lead them to repentance or enlighten their situation by clear, biblical teaching. This is a mandate for all leaders, as written in Isaiah 40:1, "Comfort ye, comfort ye my people saith your God."

Responsibility #3: Comfort: *Paramuthia*.

I Corinthians 14:3. (NKJV) But he who prophesies speaks edification and exhortation and comfort to men.

The Greek word for "comfort" — *paramuthia* — is used in this form only one time in the New Testament, here in I Corinthians 14:3. *Paramuthia* means "to speak to someone; coming close to the side of another; to watch over someone by keeping close to him; to speak to someone in a friendly way." It also carries the idea of "stimulating someone, to spur them to action, to inspire them to courage, and to urge them to a definite decision." In some contexts of Greek language, the meaning conveyed was that of speaking warning to a person, to warn them of coming danger, or of something they were doing that would cause them harm. Finally, *paramuthia* was also used in the financial world for the compensation or return of a loan, or interest satisfied.

Responsibility #4. Revelation. *Apokalupsis*.

I Corinthians 14:6. (NKJV) But now, brethren, if I come to you speaking with tongues, what shall I profit you unless I speak to you either by revelation, by knowledge, by prophesying, or by teaching?

The feeding ministry of the pastor, the "imparting" of spiritual truths, is vitally important to the success of corporate gatherings as described in the following passages:

Luke 2:32	Galatians 2:2
Romans 2:5, 16:25	Ephesians 1:17
Romans 8:19	Ephesians 3:3
I Corinthians 1:7	II Thessalonians 1:7
I Corinthians 14:6, 26	I Peter 1:13
II Corinthians 12:1, 7	I Peter 4:13
Galatians 1:12	Revelation 1:1

The Greek definition of *apokalupsis* is "to impart, declare, make manifest, disclose; an uncovering, a laying bare, making naked." It is also used about events "by which things or states or persons hitherto withdrawn from view are made visible to all, a manifestation or appearance." In addition, *apokalupsis* carries with it the idea of "something that has been in hiding, buried in the earth, that which has been covered, but now is revealed; one coming forth publicly with his view."

In each corporate gathering, we pastors or spiritual overseers of the meeting should move the people to a place of illumination through our own preaching or teaching. Biblical concepts that are hidden from the congregations' understanding should be revealed and made clear. Illumination is obviously connected to the ministry of the Holy Spirit. As we carry out our office of shepherd/teacher at corporate gatherings we should be asking ourselves: Does our ministry from the Word illuminate or conceal the truth? Do we enlighten people's understanding, or do we preach "dark sayings" and parables that cannot be understood? Is our preaching obscure, or do we use simple language and practical illustrations that people can understand and readily apply to their lives?

As we summarize the ideal of revelation, we must say that it implies not just imparting knowledge, but the actual unveiling of hidden truth. Revelation, in our context, is the *effective* transmission of *truth* to the hearers by the pastor or minister.

Responsibility #5: Knowledge: *Gnosis.*

I Corinthians 14:6. (NKJV) But now brethren, If I come to you speaking with tongues, what shall I profit you unless I speak to you either by revelation, by knowledge, by prophesying, or by teaching?

The Bible speaks specifically about knowledge in the following passages:

Romans 15:14	II Corinthians 6:6
I Corinthians 1:5	II Corinthians 8:7
I Corinthians 8:1, 7, 10-11	Colossians 2:3
I Corinthians 13:2, 8	II Peter 1:5

The Greek work *gnosis* means "to bring understanding that causes a person to enter into the truth being taught; to cause people to grasp personally a truth, which results in strong convictions that order and adjust a way of thinking."

Luke 11:52 is a key scripture to the concept of *gnosis* as used in the Greek culture. Jesus says that the Pharisees ". . . have taken away the key of knowledge." It was common in the days of Jesus for city officials to give keys to a special, honored person as he was brought into public office. Handing over the keys was symbolic of releasing and entrusting him with authority. When a Pharisee was ordained to office, he also was presented with a key. It symbolized his authority to open the Scriptures, to unlock the doors of hidden meaning and allow others to enter in. They were the professional interpreters of the old Testament Scriptures, especially the law. They were known to argue, debate, and suspend doctrinal or practical judgment on an issue because of one word in a sentence. People had this saying about them: "They suspended mountains from hairs." Due to their gross hypocrisy, these men eventually lost the key of knowledge and were no longer opening the door of understanding.

This is very typical of our day as well — the key of knowledge has been taken away. When this key is missing from corporate gatherings, the sheep become ignorant over a period of time. In the New Testament, there are four different aspects of ignorance:

1. Ignorance because of the lack of desire to know (I Peter 1:14);

2. Ignorance because of hardness of heart, willful stubbornness, and a closing of the mind (Ephesians 4:18);

3. Ignorance because of not being able to grasp what is being taught, or non-intentional ignorance (Hebrews 5:2);

4. Ignorance because of the lack of impartation of information or knowledge (Acts 4:13).

You and I as pastors must discern why our people are ignorant. Have the people lapsed in their reading and study habits, or could it be because the key of knowledge has been taken away? When ignorance increases more than knowledge, problems can develop such as:

• Stubborn and self-willed sheep (Psalm 32:9; Exodus 33:3; Deuteronomy 9:27; Acts 7:51; Proverbs 29:1; Matthew 11:29);

• A destroyed vineyard (Proverbs 24:30-34);

• A church with no voice or influence (Hosea 4:6);

• Sheep who do not have the knowledge of right principles for living (Jeremiah 4:2);

• People who are easily snared by satanic trickery (II Corinthians 2:11).

The Bible mandate for transferring knowledge from the leadership to the people is seen in Jeremiah 3:15, "And I will give you pastors according to mine heart, which shall feed you with knowledge and understanding."

Responsibility #6: Prophesying. *Propheteia.*

I Corinthians 14:22. (NKJV) Therefore tongues are for a sign, not to those who believe but to unbelievers; but prophesying is not for unbelievers but for those who believe.

Scriptures providing our basis for study of this principle are the following:

Matthew 13:14	I Thessalonians 5:20
Romans 12:6	I Timothy 1:18
I Corinthians 12:10	I Timothy 4:14
I Corinthians 14:6, 22	

Propheteia is "a discourse emanating from divine inspiration to declare the mind of God in any given situation, to affirm something beforehand." It also connotes the revealing of hidden things: "To speak as the voice of God, to declare openly, proclaim, make know publicly, speak with authority; to speak as an oracle."

You and I are responsible to speak the mind of God into the church service. Of course, if we haven't heard God, we cannot speak His mind! This aspect is critical to the dynamics of corporate gatherings. If we as overseers move into the realm of the prophetic spirit, we can speak the mind of God with authority into people's lives.

I Peter 4:11. (AMP) Whoever speaks [let him do it as one who utters] oracles of God.

I Peter 4:11. (MOFFATT) He must preach as one who utters the words of God.

In the Greek "oracle" means "a little word, a brief utterance." This does not necessarily mean our preaching must be short, but it does mean that we do not need a lengthy message to communicate the mind of God. If you as a pastor move into the realm of this ministry, you will be able at times to impart brief but powerful words because they are the words of God. The oracle in the Old Testament was the speaking place of God. God gave direction, rebuked sin, forgave sin, confirmed ministries, and so on, all from the oracle.

41

For further study on the oracle as it relates to speaking the Word and mind of God to a corporate gathering, see the following scriptures:

Matthew 7:28	Acts 5:28
Matthew 22:23	Acts 13:12
Mark 1:22, 27	I Corinthians 14:6, 26
Mark 12:38	II Timothy 4:2
John 7:16-17	Titus 1:9
John 18:19	Hebrews 6:2
Acts 2:42	II John 9:9-10

Responsibility #7. Doctrine. *Didache.*

I Corinthians 14:26. (NKJV) How is it then, brethren? Whenever you come together, each of you has a psalm, has a teaching, has a tongue, has a revelation, has an interpretation. Let all things be done for edification.

The Greek definition of *didache* is "teaching, clear instruction given so as to establish the instruction as a way of thinking and living." It denotes the idea of imparting carefully, line upon line, instruction into the life of the pupil. The pupil must understand in order to be taught. *Didache* also carries with it the idea of "gradual, systematic, fundamental learning; something that is imparted in stages, progressively; a teaching that yields something definite in value, something that can be easily grasped."

As leaders we are responsible to provide this quality of expression in every corporate gathering. This kind of teaching is easily comprehended and applied. Every leader must determine if he is systematically laying truth into the flock. Does the teaching have a definite value or a definite goal in mind? As the following scripture points out, teaching always procedes true reformation.

> **II Chronicles 17:7-9.** Also in the third year of his reign he sent to his princes, even to Benhail, and to Obadiah, and to Zechariah, and to Nethaneel, and to Michaiah, to teach in the cities of Judah.
>
> And with them he sent Levites, even Shemaiah, and Nethaniah, and Zebadiah, and Asahel, and Shemiromoth, and Jehonathan, and Adonijah, and Tobijah, and Tobadonijah, Levites; and with them Elishama and Jehoram, priests.
>
> And they taught in Judah, and had the book of the law of the Lord with them, and went about throughout all the cities of Judah, and taught the people.

This element for successful corporate gatherings can be realized through systematically teaching in a continuing series. Series teaching can be one of the most profitable means of *didache* in that it:

1. Provides balance and variety to the teaching;

2. Helps keep the leader from riding "hobby horses";

3. Saves time by interconnecting sermon ideas from week to week;

4. Helps the leader think in terms of long-range goals and vision for feeding the flock;

5. Saves falling into message-snatching pitfalls while bringing into focus usable material from the entire Bible and not just favorite passages;

6. Meets the specific needs of a body in a systematic way.

Snares to Avoid

Along with these seven functions that we as leaders must provide to the body, Scripture gives us potential snares to avoid. We are responsible to guard our flocks against these pitfalls by teaching on them, as well as being good examples ourselves.

Snare #1. The snare of allowing lukewarmness to prevail.

In Revelation 3:17, the Lord says the Laodicean church is lukewarm — neither cold nor hot. The Laodiceans were known for upholding the "rights of the people" versus submission to God's will and leadership. This describes our times as well. Indifference characterizes a self-centered world, not truly caring about the needs of one another or the commands of a holy God. Instead our people should be exhorted to "press toward the mark," as Paul writes in Phillipians 3:14. The Greek word for "press" means to "stretch forward, to reach by straining." Rather than holding back, God commands us to extend ourselves in worship, praise, exhortation, prayer, and all of the other facets of a public gathering.

Snare #2. The snare of allowing members to be at war with one another.

I Corinthians 1:10. . . . that there be no divisions among you; but that ye be perfectly joined together in the same mind and in the same judgment.

"Divisions" in the Greek means "rents, as in a garment, splintering of broken bones, or schisms among people." Obviously, a church marred by internal gossiping, slander, wounds, and divisions will not be functioning properly at its corporate gatherings. As leaders we must exhort the people to confess faults, forgive one another, and mend the breaches.

Matthew 18:15. Moreover if thy brother shall trespass against thee, go tell him his fault between thee and him alone: if he shall hear thee, thou hast gained thy brother.

Snare #3. The snare of imbalance.

We live in a time of extremes, of great reactions to truths, to policies, and to procedures of almost any kind. We need to avoid extremes or imbalance in our corporate gatherings. Imbalance comes when we have no clear convictions, vision, goals, biblical teaching, or commitments. Imbalance also comes when we have a wrong emphasis in our public meetings.

As leaders we must maintain a coordinated, balanced effort in our ministry to the Lord, to one another as believers, and to the world through fulfilling all seven of the leadership responsibilities: edification, exhortation, comfort, revelation, knowledge, prophecy, and doctrine. Then the flock of God is more likely to respond willingly to the principles of biblical living — individually and corporately — providing the balanced effort God requires for healthy corporate gatherings and church life.

Summary of the Seven Ingredients:

- edification
- exhortation
- comfort
- revelation
- knowledge
- prophecy
- doctrine

6

Corporate Gatherings: Congregational Responsibility

Our congregations also play an important part in promoting successful corporate gatherings. We are responsible to teach our church bodies how to fulfill their part in dynamic assemblies. As Isaiah 2:3 says, ". . .and he will teach us of His ways, and we will walk in His paths: . . ." Teaching always precedes walking in the truth which has been taught. This area of congregational attitudes and involvement in church services must become a teaching priority if the congregation is to walk in truth. There are four basic commitments for the people to fulfill in order to have successful corporate gatherings.

Responsibility #1. The people must be in attendance.

Hebrews 10:25. (AMP) Not forsaking or neglecting to assemble together [as believers], as is the habit of some people, but admonishing — warning, urging and encouraging — one another, and all the more faithfully as you see the day approaching.

(KNOX) . . . not abandoning . . . our common assembly . . .

(BERKELEY) . . . not neglecting our own church meeting . . .

(NEB) . . . not staying away from our meetings . . .

(PHILLIPS) . . . and let us not hold aloof from our church meetings

The key words in these verses — "abandoning, neglecting, holding aloof" — describe the influence of the spirit of our day. This is what many people are doing today — neglecting the corporate gatherings where they will be spiritually fed, taught, and directed in the ways of God. Yet Paul was very clear in his writings that gathering together was a mandate from God. The following exerpts from I Corinthians demonstrate his emphasis on attendance: things would happen "when" — not "if" — people were faithful in attendance to corporate gatherings:

I Corinthians 5:4. . . .when ye are gathered together. . .
I Corinthians 11:17. . . .that ye come together. . .
I Corinthians 11:18. . . .when ye come together in the church. . .
I Corinthians 11:20. . . .when ye come together in one place. . .
I Corinthians 11:33. . . .when ye come together to eat. . .
I Corinthians 14:23. . . .If therefore the whole church be come together into one place. . .
I Corinthians 14:26. . . .How is it then, brethren? when you come together. . .

Responsibility #2. The people must be committed to participation.

Christianity has been greatly influenced by our television generation. Society is accustomed to watching an event without any active participation — the "spectator mentality." The word "spectator" accurately describes many of the people in today's church services: "one who looks on; one who sees or beholds a given thing without taking an active part" (*Webster's Dictionary*). Thus dropping the "spectator mentality" and becoming an active participant in corporate gatherings is truly the challenge for all members of the body of Christ.

I Corinthians 14:26. How is it then, brethren? when ye come together, every one of you hath a psalm, hath a doctrine, hath a tongue, hath a revelation, hath an interpretation. Let all things be done unto edifying.

This verse clearly mandates *all* to participate and to become involved. Participation must become an individual commitment before God. We must not accept the "spectator mentality" of corporate gatherings. Participation is needed in prayer, worship, offerings, communion, ministry to others in need, and even saying "amen" to the Word preached. All of these should be normal activities to an active church member — encouraged by us as pastors so that the body ministers to the needs of the body.

Responsibility #3. The people must be expecting to receive.

Expectation, or faith, is one of the most important attitudes to be instilled in the people of God. Anticipation is the foundation for the moving of the Holy Spirit. The Book of Acts illustrates how powerful the principle of expectation is.

Acts 3:5. He gave heed unto them, *expecting* to receive something from them.

(WEYMOUTH) So he looked and waited, *expecting* to receive something from.

(AMP) And [the man] paid attention to them, *expecting* that he was going to get something from them.

(PHILLIPS) The man looked at them *expectantly*, hoping that they would give him something.

The common word in all these translations, "expecting," is the Greek word *prosdokao*, which means "to wait for with anticipation, to look for with hope, anxious waiting." Other scriptures illustrating this point are as follows:

Luke 3:15. And as the people were in expectation. . .
Acts 10:24. And Cornelius waited for them. . .
Acts 28:6. . . .after they had looked a great while. . .

In each of these scriptures we see the importance of expectation. The lame man in Acts 3 expected something that

49

day, and his expectation was not disappointed. This is a principle throughout Scripture. The church of God must expect to receive from the Lord what He has for them. We need to have expectation for our current pressing need, as well as for our daily situations, eagerly anticipating God's provision.

Psalm 62:5. My soul, wait thou only upon God; for my expectation is from Him.

Proverbs 23:18. For surely there is an end; and thine expectation shall not be cut off.

Responsibility #4. The people must maintain the centrality of Christ.

The congregation has the responsibility to keep Jesus the center of their lives, at the core of their thinking, so that they will respond appropriately to the presence of God in their corporate gatherings. There are at least seven ways in which we can maintain the centrality of Christ.

1. Maintain the simplicity of Christ. (II Corinthians 1:1-3)

In the Greek this means to be "without complexity, single in sincerity, unaffectedness." We are to exhort the members of our congregations to live their lives quietly before the Lord. Preserving the simplicity of our services will also help the people. We can do this by avoiding lots of announcements, procedures, and extra offerings that are not serving God's purpose for that particular meeting.

2. Allow Jesus to dress the lampstand. (Exodus 30:7-8; Matthew 25:1-8).

We are the lamps of God and should be ready to do His service at all times. Inevitably a lamp must be adjusted or have its wick trimmed to function more capably. Do the people's lamps shine brightly? Do they need to be "dressed" or "adjusted, set right, fitted"? Jesus will keep us "fit for the Master's use" if we submit to His care.

3. Value the "felt presence" of Jesus. (Psalm 51:11)

By doing this, the people will maintain the vision that God has for them and their local church body. As Colossians 2:19 commands, we are not to be beguiled from our personal vision of Jesus in the midst by teachings that deny Him: "And not holding the Head (Jesus), from which all the body by joints and bands having nourishment ministered, and knit together, increaseth with the increase of God."

4. Realize that we cannot go on without the "felt presence" of Jesus.

The nation of Israel's experience with the presence of God aptly illustrates this point. The following passage serves as a good example.

Exodus 33:12-13. (NKJV) Then Moses said to the Lord, "See, You say to me, 'Bring up this people.' But You have not let me know whom You will send with me. Yet You have said, 'I know you by name, and you have also found grace in My sight.'

"Now therefore, I pray, if I have found grace in Your sight, show me now Your way, that I may know You and that I may find grace in Your sight. And consider that this nation is Your people."

5. Recognize that it is the presence of God which makes the difference between us and the world.

Exodus 33:12-13 — (see reference in preceding point #4.)

6. Never allow substitution for the presence of the Lord Jesus.

Psalm 16:11. (NKJV) You will show me the path of life; in Your presence is fullness of joy, at Your right hand are pleasures forevermore.

7. Maintain the "felt presence" of Jesus by maintaining a true spirit of praise and worship.

Hebrews 1:5-6. (NKJV) For to which of the angels did He ever say: "You are My Son, today I have begotten You."? And again: "I will be to Him a Father, and He shall be to Me a Son"?

But when He again brings the firstborn into the world, He says, "Let all the angels of God worship Him."

Thus we see our congregations' responsibility to the success of corporate gatherings dovetails with that of ours as leaders. Their faithful attendance, commitment to participation, attitude of expectation, and maintenance of the centrality of Christ all enable them as worshipers to receive the Spirit's impartation through the leadership of the church. Together, in covenant, the complete flock of God can rise to the heights of praise, worship, wisdom, and love that God intended for His corporate body.

7

Corporate Gatherings: A Rejoicing Church

How can we describe a "rejoicing church?" What is a reliable criteria for evaluation? As a Pastor, I have it in my heart to orientate our church body to understand and grasp a concept of church life as God intended it.

I preached a series of sermons on the topic, 'The Way Church was Meant to Be.' One sermon focused on corporate gatherings as a rejoicing church. In this chapter I will establish a strong Biblical case outlining the need and purpose for joyful gatherings as rejoicing godly believers. And to add a spark of variety and illustration, I will include another perspective of a rejoicing church with a spontaneous first impression of our congregation. This vignette will help demonstrate the spirit and substance of what this book is about. I call this viewpoint spontaneous in that it is an unedited written comment offered by a new member of our church. He has recorded a scenario of "first impressions" upon entering our church for the first time. Let's listen to how he was impacted by the dynamics of a rejoicing church:

"First, let me explain where I was coming from. Yes, I was a Christian, mostly used to mainline denominations. I was new to the city, single and divorced, somewhat lonely and hungry for fellowship. Mostly, I needed someone to pray with to find peace and answers to big problems I was struggling with. Also, I had been searching for a church home to settle into. . .visiting one church after another for one year. A clerk in a photocopy shop suggested and gradually pressured me to visit Eugene Christian Fellowship. Finally, I checked out ECF, not really expecting to discover anything different than the normal disillusionment and emptiness I was accustomed to finding elsewhere.

"The first impression I noted was the crowded parking lot and numerous happy 'sharp looking' people eagerly walking toward the front entrance. *Joy was in the air.* My next impression was the greeter at the front door. He would *not* let go of my hand until he memorized my name. (Later that week he called me, wrote me a note of welcome, wanted to meet for coffee, and remembered my name the next week when I again attended this church!) This impression was genuinely unique and different than what I was encountering elsewhere. He was so sincere, positive and personal.

"Upon entering the large and spacious sanctuary, my eye quickly noted the rich and calming color scheme of how the church interior was decorated. Soft, muted serene colors of rose, brown, and powder blue communicated a plush upholstered image of comfort and class. This backdrop was filled with the activity of over a thousand people settling into the worship agenda of the morning. I could feel a tinge of anticipation.

"I nervously searched out a spot where I could sit and hopefully be an incognito spectator of this 'new church worship experience.' I sat down and tried to remain 'distant.'

"As soon as the worship music began my spirit quickened, and I knew, 'This is going to be different!' On the platform stood a handsome six-foot-plus music leader. He grinned, told us to stand, stretched out his long arms toward heaven and began singing like David must have praised God. . .with great reverence and total abandonment. At his lead, six talented back-up vocalists and a full-scale orchestra (complete with rhythm section of drums, bass, congo drum, piano, brass, reeds, strings and even a 'hot' harmonica player). Everyone began to praise the Lord in unison, in one accord . . .as one body. My emotions were pitched as uncontrolled hot tears flowed down my cheeks. I suddenly realized I was immersed in a 'real body' of praising believers. I didn't know how to respond. Part of me wanted to run and the other part said. . .'Stay, this is where I want you!'

"There have been various times in my church worship experience when I have raised my arms during worship (usually when I hoped nobody was watching me). . .but today, I could feel an urge to 'reach out unto the Lord' in both adoration and supplication. For it seemed that this was the spirit in which everyone was expressing their heart and soul as they too worshipped the Lord in song. As I looked around I could see praying people. Some with their eyes shut, others with their eyes open and looking upward with hands and arms outstretched, and most everyone, it seemed, with a Bible in their possession.

As one of the pastors made an announcement, I quickly looked around to observe the environment. On a side wall was an enormous graphic portrayal of a world map, illustrated images of people from nations throughout the world and a large caption lettered above it saying, 'Ask of Me and I will surely give the nations as thine inheritance.' It's obvious, I thought, that this church must be very serious about world missions and vision. Another image was a large painting of an achitect's rendering of what this church hoped to grow into. All of this seemed so unusual and graphic!

"Another sight that captured my attention was a dramtic display of eight brightly colored and textured banners. Big banners! Each one said something about Jehovah.

"As the choir was moving into position on the platform, my eyes became riveted to a hugh circle of oak under glass and brass lettering proclaiming **OUR GOD REIGNS!**

"You have to admit. . .with one quick swoop of scanning a sancturay, that this positive atmosphere didn't exactly look like a church. But it was! And as I relaxed and entered into the worship experience, I subconsciously noticed how happy I was. So I took a deep breath and tried to settle into the newness. This was indeed a total and sudden immersion into a body of Christians who truly seemed to enjoy singing, praising God and rejoicing in every way imaginable.

"As I was observing and sorting out all these impressions, yet another unexpected surprise came into being.

"The Pastor of the church, Frank Damazio, greeted everyone warmly and in a routine way directed everyone to reach out and introduce themselves to one another. As this began to happen, instantly he added, 'Please pray that God's power will minister during the service and pray for each other.'

"My one wish was to become invisible and disappear. I felt threatened! My usual stance was to remain anonymous, unnoticed and uninvolved in a church service. My shield was shattered. I responded to several people who were reaching out to me. Reluctantly, I shook hands, introduced myself and asked for prayers that my elderly and sickly step-dad would be saved (our family had been praying this prayer for 40 years. To my surprise he accepted Christ as his Savior during the following week!)...and prayed with others about their needs and dreams. As the music, smiles, preaching of God's word, and corporate 'intimacy' continued, I could feel a warm secure glow within...and made note of the image that reminded me I needed more of this! I could not understand exactly what was happening...but it agreed with everything in me that longed for more of God and my special place in the Body of Christ.

"As I walked out of the church into the sunshine and headed for my car, I could feel my battered faith uplifted and a smile on my face. I knew I would be back...maybe for good!"

Psalm 145:7. (NIV) They will *celebrate* your abundant goodness and *joyfully sing* of your righteousness.

Acts 2:46. Several versions say, "They ate, then went with gladness," "simple-hearted gladness," "great happiness," "simply joy," "unaffected joy."

I think this believer's report of his multiple first-impression contact with our corporate gathering is a present day testimony of the way church was meant to be. It is a fact that Bible historians agree the church of the first century was indeed a *happy church*! The Bible says they were glad, joyful, and celebrated God's abundant goodness.

Early Christians were happy and wanted everyone to know it! The image of the Christian life should not be associated with gloom. The godless philosopher Nietzche said, "Christians would have to look more saved if they hoped to persuade anyone!" If Christianity does not make us happy, it will not make us anything! If we are to be known as joyful people then the trademark of all Christians and churches should be consistent enthusiasm, joy and true happiness. St. Augustine said, "In the house of God there is a never-ending festival, the angel choir makes eternal holiday, the presence of God's face gives joy that never fails. And from that everlasting perpetual festivity there sounds in the ears of the heart a strain: mysterious, melodious, sweet — *provided* the *world does not drown it.*

As we continue to read about the early church in Acts, we see evidence of vibrant power of the Holy Spirit releasing His joy in the first breath of the church's new life.

Read Acts 2:28; 8:8; 13:52; 15:3, 31; 20:24; 16:34.

Defining Biblical and Non-Biblical Joy

To grasp a firm understanding of Biblical joy we need to first define what is counterfeit. The Word reminds us God wants to see His children happy, but when we move "in the flesh" to make ourselves happy in some self-centered way, we rapidly diminish our capacity to know godly joy. Even natural joy will eventually escape us.

As we examine the world's view of happiness, all we see is self gratification, the pursuit of cheap thrills and the constant search for new excitement that produces pleasure. Hedonism is defined as "natural gratification, satisfaction of lust, passion, pleasure for its own sake."

When pleasure seeking becomes a central passion, it soon escalates until it dominates our lives. The obsession for pleasure subtly enslaves us as we become worn out trying to feed uncontrolled cravings that can never be satisfied. A narcissistic society is where people love themselves and live for the moment. Stimulation is man's mandate and root motive in life. He chooses to forget the value of long-range goals. Selfish desires for personal satisfaction means exploiting and taking advantage of others. God's Word trumpets a warning alarm to beware of these pitfalls:

I Timothy 5:5,6. (KJV) But she that liveth in pleasure is dead while she liveth!

Proverbs 21:17. (KJV) He that loveth pleasure shall be a poor man.

Luke 8:14. . . . the cares and riches and pleasures of this life choke the seed!

True Joy is Biblical Joy

How do we define the meaning of joy in the pages of this book? Very difficult, to say the least! An old Scottish woman is quoted saying, "better felt than telt!" Let's further explore the meaning of joy.

Definition. The dictionary definition of joy is, "The *passion* or *emotion* excited by the acquisition of *expectation of good*; that excitement of pleasurable feelings which is caused by success, as in living according to God's divine principles, true joy comes from serving the only true God." We can derive simple logic from this definition by comparing the joy or pleasure generated by self-indulgence with the kingdoms of this world, which are passing away. Compare this joy with the "Joy of the Lord." The joy Jesus Christ gives the believer is directly connected with the Kingdom of God which never passes away. The essential difference between these two "joys" is that self-generated joy is *temporary* while joy released under the Lordship of Christ is *permanent*.

"Joy is never in our power and pleasure is. I doubt anyone who has tasted joy would ever, if both were in his power, exchange it for all the pleasures in the world." (C.S. Lewis)

We find further explanations of Biblical joy by researching the archives of Greek and Hebrew definitions. There are three main groups of words in the New Testament which denote human joy and happiness.

Chairo — To be filled with intense joy, physical comfort and well being. The basis of this joy is to be rejoicing over the mercy and grace of God working in someone's life other than our own.

Euphraino — The Old Testament meaning of this word indicates the subjective feeling of joy, to be inwardly glad. The New Testament non-subjective meaning of this word denotes the joy of festive company.

Agalliaomai — The outward demonstration of joy and exultation experienced in public worship. To rejoice, overflow, adore, honor, glorify. To make a show, boast jubilant rejoicing as in a festival activity and atmosphere. Rejoicing that arises from gratification and unshakable trust in the God who has constantly helped us and is *still* helping His people today.

Purging away the counterfeit happiness influenced by humanism and selfishness and merging the root meanings of *Chairo, Euphraino* and *Agalliaomai* under the Lordship of Jesus Christ lays the groundwork for a foundation upon which a rejoicing church can invite and experience the presence of God.

"Joy is the most infallible sign of the presence of God." (Bloy)

Foundations for Genuine Biblical Joy

As we muse upon the true nature of Biblical joy, we find that although it is emotional, it must be soundly established upon a clear understanding of one's right relationship with God. We need to jettison habits and patterns of superficial stimuli. We can no longer be conformed to the ways of the world for there are no substitutes for the deep foundations of genuine joy. The force of righteousness emerges from joy that has its roots deep into God. This godly brand of joy is not affected by moods, circumstances, seasons, fears, people or things.

Romans 14:17. (KJV) For the kingdom of God is. . . righteousness, peace and joy in the Holy Ghost.

(KNOX) The kingdom of God is. . . rightness of heart, finding our peace and joy in the Holy Spirit.

Four Foundation Truths

God's Word provides four building blocks establishing a firm foundation upon which the church can be a holy atmosphere where people can encounter the living God.

Foundation #1. Someone once said, "If you can't find God, guess who moved?" The first building block is the turning to God and putting our trust in God.

As leaders we must set the stage for corporate worship by keeping the essential focus immediately upon God, affirming our trust in Him. Sheep will heed the shepherd's voice! They need to be gently encouraged to "unpack their baggage" and remember why they came to church. In doing so, there is a response and trust in the gospel, God's plan of forgiveness, cleansing and acceptance by the blood of Jesus. The outcome of both personal and corporate repentance and trust is the foundation block of "permanent joy."

Romans 15:13. (NIV) May the God of hope fill you with all joy and peace as you *trust* in Him, so that you may overflow with hope by the power of the Holy Spirit.

Foundation #2: It's a sin to realize God has opened a door, but refuse to enter and walk in. Entering into Kingdom living is walking into the knowledge of God and embracing His higher thoughts, ways, love and government. This requires obedience, submission and supplication, for this is not just salvation but Lordship, the second foundation block.

Romans 14:17, 18. (NAS) . . . for the kingdom of God is not eating and drinking, but righteousness and peace and joy in the Holy Spirit. For he who in this *way* serves Christ is acceptable to God and approved by men.

Foundation #3. The third important building block in a solid foundation is the establishment of a *love for righteousness* that affects the way you live. In Romans 4:17 we read the kingdom of God is righteousness which is defined in Greek meaning *"right* actions, *right* attitudes and *right* convictions." God is calling His peculiar and treasured possessions to be sanctified, i.e.: to be clean, holy and pure.

Positional Righteousness. God's people consciously need to make a decision to abandon their worldly ways and change their position to *right standing* through faith in Jesus. Not by works, or by law, but by trust in Christ, we are righteous in Him.

II Corinthians 5:21. (NAS) He made Him who knew no sin to be sin on our behalf, that we might become the righteousness of God in Him.

Practical Righteousness. Once a Christian adheres to a personal love of righteousness and accepts this position, the outgrowth is a righteous behavior resulting from a right relationship with Christ.

The flip side of this coin is where the grim concern lays hidden. When our basic understanding of and participation in righteousness is *faulty*, our peace will be disturbed resulting in mood swings and roller coaster joylessness.

Hebrews 1:9 identifies our third building block saying, "Thou hast loved righteousness and hated lawlessness, therefore God, thy God, hath anointed thee with the oil of gladness above thy companions."

Foundation #4. Pastors and other church leaders are like skilled stone masons. They envision the long-term rewards of building upon solid rock. Our fourth foundation block is the Holy Spirit Himself.

Romans 14:7, 8. (NAS) For not one of us lives for hismelf, and not one dies for himself for if we live, we live for the Lord, or if we die we die for the Lord; therefore whether we live or die, we are the Lords.

The Christian who is broken, and has died to self in the "dark night of the soul," knows that he knows he is living the "exchanged life." This foundation block is not established *in the flesh*, or *in the world*, but *in the Holy Ghost*, a life lived unto the Lord. For only the Holy Spirit in me can truly know the Holy Spirit.

Eight Characteristics Describing a Rejoicing Church

How do you spot a happy church? A rejoicing church can be identified by eight characteristics. We conclude this chapter with the harvest of God's Word seen in the outward expressions of a body of godly people who are living proof that the gospel works.

1. Rejoicing People Worship with Joy

Psalm 16:11. (NAS) Thou wilt make known to me the path of life; in Thy presence is fullness of joy; in Thy right hand there are pleasures forever.

As we examine these scriptures concerning a rejoicing people, we find that the church should worship with joy. When we worship after the Biblical model, the atmosphere is charged with the presence of the Lord; the presence of the Lord means we experience the "fullness of joy." The singing of psalms, hymns, and spiritual songs along with audible spontaneous praises sung together should all be done with "joyful lips."

Psalm 63:5. (NAS) . . . my mouth offers praises with joyful lips.

There are times in our corporate gathering when we have a "shabach," a *loud shout.* Shouting joyfully with unity of the instruments and the voices of the people is a dynamic way of proclaiming the victory of our God. There are many scriptures that tell us to use *this joyful shouting* as part of our worship experience.

Psalm 66:1. (NAS) Shout joyfully to God, all the earth; sing the glory of His name, make His praise glorious.
Psalm 95:1. (NAS) O come, let us sing for joy to the Lord; let us shout joyfully to the rock of our salvation.
Psalm 27:6. (NAS) And now my head will be lifted up above my enemies around me; and I will offer in His tent sacrifices with shouts of joy; I will sing, yes, I will sing praises to the Lord.

Psalm 32:11. (NAS) Be glad in the Lord and rejoice, you righteous ones, and shout for joy, all you who are upright in heart.

The one characteristic that is of utmost importance in our day and age is a rejoicing church with a rejoicing, celebrating worship. The world is full of depressing music, hard times, disappointments and battles. Church should be an uplifting festival of joy, led by joyful musicians, joyful song leaders, and joyful choirs as the Psalmist describes in Psalm 42:4.

Psalm 42:4. (NAS) . . . For I used to go along with the throng and lead them in procession to the house of God, with the voice of joy and thanksgiving, a multitude keeping festival.

As a rejoicing people we keep our hope in Christ, His atoning work and His second coming. We know that He is faithful to do in us and for us all that He has said. We believe in Who we cannot see and rejoice with Him we cannot touch. By faith and the power of the Holy Spirit we stand firm in our rejoicing even when we suffer wrongs.

I Peter 1:8. (NAS) And though you have not seen Him, you love Him, and though you do not see Him now, but believe in Him, you greatly rejoice with joy inexpressible and full of glory.
I Peter 4:13. (NAS) But to the degree that you share the sufferings of Christ, keep on rejoicing; so that also at the revelation of His glory, you may rejoice with exultation.

2. Rejoicing People Enjoy Their God

Probably one of the greatest criticism against the mainline church in America, and possibly around the world, is that religious people do not seem to enjoy life, themselves or their God. Trying to mortify the flesh, keep pure from the world, conquer an ever-attacking devil and deal with everyday hassles are just a few reasons why some Christians do not seem to be enjoying life, themselves or God. The Lord wants us to serve him with joy and enjoy all that He has provided for us. Many Christians serve God with great respect and to the letter obedience but do it without joy. This is not only a shame but a sin. In Luke 15:11-33 we have the story of the prodigal son who took all his inheritance, all that the father had for him and went into a far country and wasted it. The prodigal son came to himself, realized his condition, and returned to his father. The father wasted no time to restore the lost son to a place of honor; a rejoicing celebration resulted. Out came the fattened calf for a great feast with happy music and plenty of the best of the father's wine. The story is a moving emotional reminder of the father's love, but it doesn't end there. The prodigal son had an older brother who was out working in the field during this festival. When he came in from work that day, he heard music, he saw people dancing and celebrating. He immediately inquired as to what this unplanned party was all about. When he found out it was for his backslidden younger brother, he was angry and would not *enjoy* the festival with all the others. The father went out to try and reason with him and persuade him to come into the happy celebration. The older brother's response is a classic response of those who do everything for the Father year after year with detailed obedience and even sacrifice, but one ingredient is missing — they haven't *enjoyed* their God. Let us read these scriptures and evaluate ourselves.

Luke 15:29-32. (NAS) "But he answered and said to his father, 'Look! For so many years I have been serving you, and I have never neglected a command of yours; and *yet* you have never given me a kid, that I might be merry with my friends;

but when this son of yours came, who has devoured your wealth with harlots, you killed the fattened calf for him.'

"And he said to him, '*My* child, you have always been with me, and all that is mine is yours.

'But we had to be merry and rejoice, for this brother of yours was dead and *has begun* to live, and *was* lost and has been found."

The words stand out like bold print, "All that is mine is yours." The older brother could have enjoyed his father's wealth at any time. But he was so involved in serving the needs of this father's ranch that he never enjoyed his father's wealth.

Serving the Lord with joy is a command. When we neglect this aspect of God's plan and become religious like the Pharisees, the outward becomes more important than the inward and results in hypocrisy. This is what so many young people rebel against, not true Christianity but joyless religion. When parents and leaders lose their power to *enjoy* their God and their church, they lose the power to lead.

Deuteronomy 28:47. (NAS) Because you did not serve the Lord your God with joy and a glad heart, for the abundance of all things; . . .

Psalm 36:8-9. (NAS) They drink their fill of the abundance of Thy house; and Thou dost give them to drink of the river of Thy delights. For with Thee is the foundation of life; in Thy light we see light.

Romans 5:11. (NAS) And not only this, but we also exult in God through our Lord Jesus Christ, through whom we have now received the reconciliation.

Psalm 5:11. (NAS) But let all who take refuge in Thee be glad, let them sing for joy; and mayest Thou shelter them, that those who love Thy name shall exult in Thee.

Psalm 35:9. (NAS) And my soul shall rejoice in the Lord; it shall exult in His salvation.

---

3. Rejoicing People Know How to Laugh

When you put sound to joy it will come out as laughter, just as sorrow manifests itself in crying. Laughter is joy flowing. If you have lost your laughter, your relationship with the Lord may be suffering. Laughter is God's gift to us to enable us to enjoy all of life's surprises. According to Dr. Ean Crocker of Sydney, Australia, those who find it easy to laugh seldom have heart attacks. It's the anxious soul that is always up tight, which strains the inner life, destroying both body and soul. If laughter could be ordered at the corner drug store, doctors would prescribe many laughs a day! Laughter is the joyful sound that should be heard in any gathering of God's people.

Psalm 89:15. (NAS) How blessed are the people who know the joyful sound! O Lord, they walk in the light of Thy countenance.

The dynamics of corporate gatherings are found in this basic attitude that must be developed in the people of God. Thanksgiving, a grateful attitude for all that He has done will result in a joyful atmosphere that will allow people to laugh and rejoice. Psalm 126 is a psalm of thanksgiving and a psalm that displays the ingredients of a dynamic corporate gathering.

Psalm 126:1-6. (NAS) When the Lord brought back the captive ones of Zion, we were like those who dream.
Then our mouth was filled with *laughter*, and our tongue with joyful shouting; then they said among the nations, "The Lord has done great things for them."
The Lord has done great things for us; we are glad.
Restore our captivity, O Lord, as the streams in the South.
Those who sow in tears shall reap with *joyful shouting*.
He who goes to and fro weeping, carrying his bag of seed, shall indeed come again with a *shout of joy*, bringing his sheaves with him. (Emphasis added)

Rejoicing people know how to laugh and be merry. This, according to scripture, not only lifts the spirit but actually ministers to the physical body.

Proverbs 17:22. (KJV) A merry heart doeth good like a medicine, but a broken spirit drieth the bones.
A rejoicing heart doeth good to the body.

A joyful heart worketh an excellent cure.
A cheerful heart makes a quick recovery.

4. Rejoicing People Rejoice Independent of Circumstances

In the world, people get happy when good things happen to them. Maybe it's a raise of salary at their job, a special party for them, a new-found relationship. But it also can be short-lived rejoicing if the circumstances happen to change, especially if they change for the worse. Rejoicing is then turned into sorrow or even depression. If our rejoicing is linked to our circumstances, we may well be on the road to a very moody lifestyle. Jesus taught us in his great sermon on the mount how to respond to adverse treatment from the world.

Matthew 5:11-12. (NAS) "Blessed are you when men cast insults at you, and persecute you, and say all kinds of evil against you falsely, on account of Me.
"Rejoice, and be glad, for your reward in heaven is great, for so they persecuted the prophets who were before you."

The Apostle Paul sets the example as a great model for us to follow in this rejoicing principle. Paul never let circumstance dictate his response. His inner man never allowed the outer man to dictate his mood, or his level of joy. His rejoicing was independent of his circumstances.

Acts 16:22-26. (NAS) And the crowd rose up together against them, and the chief magistrates tore their robes off them, and proceeded to order them to be beaten with rods.
And when they had inflicted many blows upon them, they threw them in prison, commanding the jailer to guard them securely;
and he, having received such a command, threw them into the inner prison, and fastened their feet in the stocks.
But about midnight Paul and Silas were praying and singing hymns of praise to God, and the prisoners were listening to them;

and suddenly there came a great earthquake, so that the foundations of the prison house were shaken; and immediately all the doors were opened, and everyone's chains were unfastened.

II Corinthians 4:8-10. (NAS) We are afflicted in every way, but not crushed; perplexed, but not despairing;

persecuted, but not forsaken; struck down, but not destroyed;

always carrying about in the body the dying of Jesus, that the life of Jesus also may be manifested in our body.

II Corinthians 4:16-18. (NAS) Therefore we do not lose heart, but though our outer man is decaying, yet our inner man is being renewed day by day.

For momentary, light affliction is producing for us an eternal weight of glory far beyond all comparison,

while we look not at the things which are seen, but at the things which are not seen; for the things which are seen are temporal, but the things which are not seen are eternal.

II Corinthians 7:5-6. (NAS) For even when we came into Macedonia our flesh had no rest, but we were afflicted on every side: conflicts without, fears within.

But God, who comforts the depressed, comforted us by the coming of Titus;

II Corinthians 11:23-28. (NAS) Are they servants of Christ? (I speak as if insane) I more so; in far more labors, in far more imprisonments, beaten times without number, often in danger of death.

Five times I received from the Jews thirty-nine lashes.

Three times I was beaten with rods, once I was stoned, three times I was shipwrecked, a night and a day I have spent in the deep.

I have been on frequent journeys, in dangers from rivers, dangers from robbers, dangers from my countrymen, dangers from the Gentiles, dangers in the city, dangers in the wilderness, dangers on the sea, dangers among false brethren;

I have been in labor and hardship, through many sleepless nights, in hunger and thirst, often without food, in cold and exposure.

Apart from such external things, there is the daily pressure upon me of concern for all the churches.

═══

Paul truly learned to be victorious in whatsoever state or circumstance he found himself in. This principle of rejoicing is a discipline to develop through life. It won't be easy at first, but eventually it will become a spiritual habit, an automatic response.

Philippians 4:11. (NAS) Not that I speak from want; for I have learned to be content in whatever circumstances I am.

Philippians 4:4. (NAS) Rejoice in the Lord always; again I say, rejoice!

I Thessalonians 5:16-18. (NAS) Rejoice always; pray without ceasing;

in everything give thanks; for this is God's will for you in Christ Jesus.

Habakkuk 3:17-18. (NAS) Though the fig tree should not blossom, and there be no fruit on the vines, though the yield of the olive should fail, and the fields produce no food, though the flock should be cut off from the fold, and there be no cattle in the stalls,

Yet I will exult in the Lord, I will rejoice in the God of my salvation.

II Corinthians 7:4. (NAS) Great is my confidence in you, great is my boasting on your behalf; I am filled with comfort. I am overflowing with joy in all our affliction.

5. Rejoicing People are Strong in the Lord

Nehemiah 8:9-10. (NAS) Then Nehemiah, who was the governor, and Ezra the priest and scribe, and the Levites who taught the people said to all the people, "This day is holy to the Lord your God; do not mourn or weep." For all the people were weeping when they heard the words of the law.

Then he said to them, "Go, eat of the fat, drink of the sweet, and send portions to him who has nothing prepared; for this day is holy to our Lord. Do not be grieved, for the joy of the Lord is your strength."

The exhortation given here in Nehemiah by Ezra the scribe, the Levites and Nehemiah serves as a theme text for all corporate gatherings. When we come together, it is a *Holy Day,* a day to put away mourning and weeping. When we come together, it is a time "to eat the fat, drink of the sweet and send portions to him who has nothing prepared." The gatherings of God's people should be turned into a joyful celebration — not a sorrowful service. Some church services lean so heavily on convicting people of their sins that condemnation is the result. This does not strengthen the people of God; it weakens them. The exhortation in this text is, "The *joy* of the Lord is your strength!" Adam Clarke, a Bible commentator, says it well: "Religious joy, properly tempered with continual dependence on the help of God, meekness of mind, and self-deference, is a powerful means of strengthening the soul. In such a state every duty is practical, every duty is delightful. In such a frame of mind no man ever fell, and in such a state of mind the general health of the body is much improved; a cheerful heart is not only a continual feast, but also a continual medicine."

The dynamics of a corporate gathering is realized by the ingredients we put in. Those who lead the public service should hold such a philosophy. The *joy* of the Lord is the strength of this gathering. How can we be instruments to facilitate this joy into reality? Time in prayer and meditating on special portions of scripture should be the duty of every worship leader before he or she ever leads a service. Every corporate gathering should see the results as recorded in Nehemiah 8:12.

Nehemiah 8:12. (NAS) And all the people went away to eat, to drink, to send portions and to celebrate the great festival, because they understood the words which had been made known to them.

---

6. Rejoicing People Weep Without Despair

As we have considered the corporate gathering to be a celebration of joy and rejoicing, filled with laughter and singing, let me hasten to say there are also times of weeping. The corporate gathering can experience all the seasons and moods of God with great benefit. Ecclesiastes 3:1-8 sets out what I call the rainbow of experiences that may come to a corporate gathering.

Ecclesiastes 3:1-8. (NAS) There is an appointed time for everything. And there is a time for every event under heaven—
A time to give birth, and a time to die;
A time to plant, and a time to uproot what is planted.
A time to kill, and a time to heal.
A time to tear down, and a time to build up.
A time to weep, and a time to laugh;
A time to mourn, and a time to dance.
A time to throw stones, and a time to gather stones;
A time to embrace, and a time to shun embracing.
A time to search, and a time to give up as lost;
A time to keep, and a time to throw away.
A time to tear apart, and a time to sew together;
A time to be silent, and a time to speak.
A time to love, and a time to hate;
A time for war, and a time for peace.

If you have been a part of God's church for any length of time, you have experienced or heard of these many different seasons of God's people. Weeping may be a part of our experiences especially when there is the time "to tear apart," or "a time to give up as lost." To weep when God is working deep within the inner fibers of the church is absolutely right. But we must not weep as those who have no hope. We weep with faith. We weep with purpose. We know that our weeping is like the winter; it will pass and spring will come.

Song of Solomon 2:11-12. (NAS) For behold, the winter is past, the rain is over and gone.
The flowers have already appeared in the land; the time has arrived for pruning the vines, and the voice of the turtledove has been heard in our land.

We know that our weeping is like the night; it will pass and the morning sun will come. We weep with hope.

> **Psalm 30:5.** (NAS) Weeping may last for the night but a shout of joy comes in the morning.
> (KNOX) Sorrow is but a guest of the night but joy comes in the morning.
> (DEW) In the morning comes a song of joy.

We know that our tears are not shed in vain but shed in faith, and faith like a seed will bring forth a harvest in due season.

> **Psalm 126:5-6.** (NAS) Those who sow in tears shall reap with joyful shouting.
> He who goes to and fro weeping, carrying his bag of seed, shall indeed come again with a shout of joy, bringing his sheaves with him.

7. Rejoicing People Rejoice as an Act of Their Will

Over and over again we read in the Psalms the words *"I will."* These two words speak of soul discipline in the habit of worship. Soul discipline is the act of bringing your will into godly submission and the act of bringing your soul into godly obedience.

> **Psalm 9:1.** (NAS) I will give thanks to the Lord with all my heart;
> I will tell of Thy wonders.
> I will be glad and exult in Thee;
> I will sing praise to Thy name, O Most High.

The "I will" of rejoicing is the key to continual dynamic rejoicing in our corporate celebration. We must teach and practice soul discipline in the habit of worship.

> **Psalm 42:5,11.** (NAS) Why are you in despair, O my soul? And why have you become disturbed within me? Hope in God, for I shall again praise Him for the help of His presence.

Why are you in despair, O my soul? And why have you become disturbed within me? Hope in God, for I shall yet praise Him, the help of my countenance, and my God.

Psalm 13:5,6. (NAS) But I have trusted in Thy lovingkindness; my heart shall rejoice in Thy salvation.

I will sing to the Lord, because He has dealt bountifully with me.

Psalm 31:7. (NAS) I will rejoice and be glad in Thy lovingkindness, because Thou hast seen my affliction; Thou hast known the troubles of my soul.

Psalm 34:1. (NAS) I will bless the Lord at all times; His praise shall continually be in my mouth.

---

8. *Rejoicing People Love to Rise to Faith Challenges*

I can recall attending a church service when the pastor was challenging the people to arise and build a new sanctuary. The response was anything but electric! The people listened passively with no seeming faith response at all. Hard to understand? No! If you would have been in that corporate gathering, you would understand why there was so little faith-response in the people. There was no joy in the singing, no worship in the worship service. The spiritual flow was almost non-existent. Why should they arise and do anything when the spiritual climate in the church was below freezing! Faith and obedience flow out from a rejoicing spirit. When there is joy and rejoicing in the believers' hearts, rising to the challenges before them is basically an easy step to take. When our corporate gathering becomes a rejoicing celebration, faith will flow like a mighty river. Not a superficial, manipulated faith but a true inner conviction that God can do anything. When God is exalted in our worship with an emphasis on His power, His faithfulness, His ability to do exceedingly abundantly above all we ask or think, faith is automatic. A rejoicing church will always respond to challenges with a, "Yes, we are more than able to move that mountain." Dr. Peter Wagner speaks of the third generation slippage in the 25- to 35-year-old churches. This is when the church is not moving in the same spirit of faith that it had in the early years. How do we avoid this spiritual death? I believe the attitude and faith of a rejoicing people will always stay fresh and be ready to rise to the challenge when they adopt the "Caleb perspective."

Numbers 13:30. (NAS) Then Caleb quieted the people before Moses, and said, "We should by all means go up and take possession of it, for we shall surely overcome it.

Numbers 14:6-8. (NAS) And Joshua the son of Nun and Caleb the son of Jephunneh, of those who had spied out the land, tore their clothes;

and they spoke to all the congregation of the sons of Israel, saying, "The land which we passed through to spy out is an exceedingly good land.

"If the Lord is pleased with us, then He will bring us into this land, and give it to us — a land which flows with milk and honey."

Philippians 1:25. (NAS) And convinced of this, I know that I shall remain and continue with you all for your progress and joy in the faith.

Hebrews 12:2. (NAS) Fixing our eyes on Jesus, the author and perfecter of faith, who for the joy set before Him endured the cross, despising the shame, and has sat down at the right hand of the throne of God.

The attitude portrayed here is one that will always do great things for God. Let us arise and take our Canaan Land with a Caleb attitude. He truly is a Biblical optimist.

Summary

Throughout the fabric of these many scriptures we see the red thread of joyous celebration as a mandate for any and all conditions. As I personally continue to meditate upon the Word of God and respond to the leading of the Holy Spirit, I am convinced we are seeing a revelation of how church was meant to be. As pastors and church leaders we are therefore responsible to our Chief Shepherd to set forth these Biblical principles as guidelines to help our corporate gatherings become a rejoicing celebration. As people become accustomed to this way of worship, they will become more expectant to receive. . .yes, even the presence of God.

8

Corporate Gatherings: A Positive Experience

A celebrating church can be a positive experience! I believe there is only one way to all the treasures of God, and that is the triumphant way of faith. For it is by faith alone that we enter into a knowledge of the attributes of God, become partakers of His provisions and participate in the spiritual life. Perhaps the greatest outgrowth of a celebrating church is the infusion of the faith of God into the receptive hearts of a people who joyously worship Him.

Hebrews 10:19-22. (NAS) Since therefore, brethren, we have confidence to enter the holy place by the blood of Jesus,
by a new and living way which He inaugurated for us through the veil, that is, His flesh,
and since we have a great priest over the house of God,
let us draw near with a sincere heart in full assurance of faith. . .

Considering these perilous times equal the evil nature of the Babylonian history, there is nothing more needed in the lives of people than a celebrating church where worship and preaching firms up our faith. Hebrews 10 speaks of a faith that *receives*. Hebrews 11 speaks of a faith that *triumphs*. And Hebrews 12 speaks of a faith that *finishes*. It is with this bold note of faith that I conclude the final chapter of *The Dynamics of Corporate Gathering*. There is nothing in this world more dynamic than the mystery of faith. The questions then unfold: "What is faith and how do we appropriate it?" "Do we really understand the power we have in the name and blood of Christ?"

The concept of faith is highlighted in the Epistle of Hebrews. The writer of Hebrews speaks in this passage of great eloquence and power, unfolding the concept of faith. The full spectrum of this message is a bright focus upon faith as *Total Trust in God.* Total trust enables the believer to press on steadfastly, confronting whatever lessons the seasons of life bring about.

In Hebrews 11, the writer selects a magnificent host of faith heroes from the Old Testament and briefly shows how faith *motivated* all of them and *led them forward,* no matter how difficult or impossible the circumstances were. Every faith hero has dared to believe the unseen and trust a promise . . . things for which they had to wait and hope. The kinships that knitted this great network of believers together was faith.

As responsible pastors and church leaders of God's flock, I believe we should orchestrate our corporate gatherings in such a way to train and condition Olympic Christians. Every week people come to church seeking fellowship with other Christians. They come reaching out to know God better. They come with varying needs, dreams, goals, hopes and hurts. But perhaps the single most common thread evidenced in the lives of Christians every week is that they come to church with a *strained faith.*

The steadfast plea of the Psalmist teaches us to pray. . . , *"life is tough, God is good!"* Life *is* tough for those who walk by faith, not by sight. Faith is strained by the pressures of life. By facing the adverse and being victimized by the world's

78

influence; faith is strained in the struggle with satanic snares, unanswered prayers and contradictions. People are weary from bearing the bondage of burdens of broken relationships, ill-health and financial defeat. We see people entering the church sanctuary to worship the living Savior, beaten and worn thin from long-suffering and continual fatigue.

The mark of leadership is to see and meet the needs of people from a biblical viewpoint.

I Thessalonians 3:5. "I sent to know your faith. . ."(AMP) "How you were standing the strain and endurance of your faith." (WEY) "To know the true condition of your faith."

To be *strained* is to stretch, be overtaxed, to struggle, travail and suffer with pain. I Thessalonians 3:1-4, 2:9 bring forth several primary pressures and difficulties of life that pressurize and overstretch faith until it is strained.

1. *Afflictions:* To be afflicted is to be maltreated and tormented; to suffer adversity and hardship.
2. *Tribulations:* The suffering of tribulations is to be pressed hard; to suffer and be miserable due to the intense pressure of circumstances.
3. *Labor and Travail:* The toil and hardship of stress-causing conditions brings wear and tear on body, mind and spirit. Continued labor and struggle drains the essence and joy of life as one struggles to overcome difficulties.
4. *Satanic hinderances:* The subtle and deceitful tactics of evil aims to cut into and impede one's course of action until progress is hindered with countless real or imagined obstacles.

I Thessalonians 3:3. . . . that no man should be moved by these afflictions.

79

(RHM) . . . might be shrinking back in these tribulations, should not waver in these circumstances.

The end result of *strain* is a weakened faith that begins to shrink! As we evaluate the spiritual temperature of our congregations, a proper diagnosis would be the recognition of *shrinking faith*. A sober mandate of the Word reminds us, "God has no pleasure in him that shrinks back" Hebrews 10:35-39.

As we cooperate with and submit to the guidance of the Holy Spirit, He will help leadership detect and uncover defective faith.

I Thessalonians 3:10. ". . . might perfect that which is lacking in your faith?"

". . . might adjust the defects of your faith whatever is lacking, imperfect and needed."

The Apostle Paul's desire was to correct, restore, and equip the Thessalonians in respect to their faith. Paul felt his presence could foster their defective faith. This is truly the desired outcome of each corporate gathering.

As spiritual servants, our purpose is to discover what is lacking in the believer's faith and supply the missing parts. The Greek word for "lacking" in I Thessalonians 3:10 is "husterema" which means, "a deficiency, inadequate, insufficient, to be inferior, that which comes behind, failing to reach the goal."

Defective faith can cause failure

On the bright, cheerful morning of January 28, 1986, the lives of the brave Challenger Space Explorer crew were suddenly ended due to defective O-rings parts in the rocket systems.

The potential productivity of faith is an inherent, latent power that comes with every supernatural seed God gives the believer. Like the Challenger, this power is designed to work. Defective action or reaction in an individual can cause failure and stop the productivity of the seed. The outcome is death and destruction. Jesus says in Luke 22:31,32, "Satan desires to sift you . . . but I have prayed that thy *faith fail not.*"

Faith is supposed to work and *can* work extraordinary miracles for everyone. Let's examine the meaning of defectiveness.

Definition of the term Defective: "The want or absence of something necessary or useful towards perfection; defect in seeing or hearing; defect in timber or in an instrument." In the realm of faith, a *defective faith* has to do with its short-coming. It simply does not quite make the grade and falls short of the mark. Something is missing and is not working correctly when it should be producing.

The model Champion for Christ is St. Paul whose desire was always to correct, admonish, restore and equip the believers in respect to faith. As one hand washes the other, Paul felt his presence could foster their defective faith. In like manner, when the strong and weak mix and gather together for worship and study of God's Word, the aura and fragrance of faith enhances a lacking faith.

Seven Characteristics of a Defective Faith

There are seven keys that will open doors behind which hide the destructive forces hindering a vibrant faith. Unlock these doors and you see why and how people become fearful and are hesitant in trusting, allowing and encouraging God to reign in their lives.

1. *Defective faith is the result of a lack of God's Word*

81

Romans 10:17. (NAS) So faith comes from hearing, and hearing by the word of Christ.

The Word is faith. It is the source of all faith. As a house plant weakens from the lack of water, so does faith weaken without a constant supply of God's Word.

Colossians 3:16. (NAS) Let the word of Christ richly dwell within you, with all wisdom teaching and admonishing one another with psalms and hymns and spiritual songs, singing with thankfulness in your hearts to God.

Revelation 12:11. (NAS) And they overcame him because of the blood of the Lamb and because of the word of their testimony, and they did not love their life even to death.

The dynamics of corporate worship is energized by the proclaiming of the Word.

2. Defective faith is a result of sense-ruled believing and a sense-dominated faith.

John 20:24-29. (NAS) But Thomas, one of the twelve, called Didymus, was not with them when Jesus came.

The other disciples therefore were saying to him, "We have seen the Lord!" But he said to them, "Unless I shall see in His hands the imprint of the nails, and put my finger into the place of the nails, and put my hand into His side, I will not believe."

And after eight days again His disciples were inside, and Thomas with them. Jesus came, the doors having been shut, and stood in their midst, and said, "Peace be with you."

Then He said to Thomas, "Reach here your finger, and see my hands; and reach here your hand, and put it into My side; and be not unbelieving, but believing."

Thomas answered and said to Him, "My Lord and my God!"

Jesus said to him, "Because you have seen Me, have you believed? Blessed are they who did not see, and yet believed."

Sense knowledge holds fast to the confession of the physical evidence whereas faith holds fast to the Word of God. Abraham was one of the best examples of a man who was not ruled by sense knowledge. Abraham did not let his sense knowledge rob him of God's promise, even when his body said it was impossible. He didn't look at the deadness of his own body but believed in the promise of the Word of God. We have learned to trust so utterly in our eyes, our ears and our senses that spiritual things are hard to understand.

Romans 4:19-21. (NAS) And without becoming weak in faith he contemplated his own body, now as good as dead since he was about a hundred years old, and the deadness of Sarah's womb;

Yet, with respect to the promise of God, he did not waver in unbelief, but grew strong in faith, giving glory to God,

and being fully assured that what He had promised, He was able also to perform.

The dynamics of corporate gatherings is conditioned by an emphasis upon the Word and not by the five physical senses.

3. *Defective faith is the result of believing in your experience more than in God and His Word.*

II Corinthians 5:7. (NAS) for we walk by faith, not by sight —

When experiences become our standard, the human spirit is honored. Experience seekers are always unstable. The dynamics of corporate gatherings are reverenced when experiences bow to The Word.

4. *Defective faith is the result of wrong confession and negative confession.*

> **Hebrews 4:14.** (NAS) Since then we have a great high priest, who has passed through the heavens, Jesus the Son of God, let us hold fast our confession.

Your believing can take opposite forms. It can be faith or it can be doubt. The confession of faith via right confession can be the key to everything! Whatever you can conceive by the works of the Holy Spirit and believe, you can do!

A wrong confession is one of defeat, failure, doubt, fear and weakness.

> **Romans 10:10.** (NAS) For with the heart man believes, resulting in righteousness, and with the mouth he confesses, resulting in salvation.

The dynamics of corporate gatherings rise only to the exact height of the believer's confession. Success comes in cans. . . not in can'ts. Don't say you can't when God says you can!

5. *Defective faith is the result of an unforgiving spirit.*

Matthew 18:35 expresses the sobering conviction of our Father's heart, "So shall my heavenly Father also do to you, if each of you does not forgive his brother from your heart." The sin of unforgiveness produces a spiritual dryrot caused by fear. Fear destroys and blocks the rivers of faith. The dynamics of corporate gatherings releases faith when the body of Christ forgives one another.

6.*Defect faith confuses hope with faith.*

What is the major difference between hope and faith? Hope is for tomorrow. . . in the *future* while faith is for *right*

84

now, today! The meaning of faith is found in Hebrews 11:1 which says, "Faith is the assurance of things hoped for, a conviction of things not seen." Hope has no substance. Hope is the anchor of the soul, dependent upon faith. You can have hope without faith, but you cannot have faith without hope. Faith is the engine and hope is the caboose.

Mark 11:24. (NAS) Therefore I say to you, all things for which you pray and ask, believe that you have received them, and they shall be granted you.

The dynamics of corporate gatherings are people vibrant with the faith of Jehovah, the God of *right now.*

7. *Defective faith resulting from human reasoning that wars against faith in the spirit.*

II Corinthians 10:3-5. (NAS) For though we walk in the flesh, we do not war according to the flesh,
for the weapons of our warfare are not of the flesh, but divinely powerful for the destruction of fortresses.
We are destroying speculations and every lofty thing raised up against the knowledge of God, and we are taking every thought captive to the obedience of Christ

---

Human reasoning can conjure up a mirage of illusion that resembles truth. These delusions are frauds, deceptions and are empowered by the angel of light who masquerades righteousness to trick us.

Human thinking is death to the spirit of faith. We live in an era of humanism where the idols of the high places are the great resources and philosophies of the world.

The dynamics of corporate gatherings are powerful in the casting down of imaginings, pulling down of strongholds and denouncing every lying thought of the devil.

85

It is in this context we see an image of the dynamics of corporate gatherings being comprised of a bruised and ragged flock of sheep coming under the firm and loving care of the Chief Shepherd, Jesus Christ. With this hopeful perspective, our minds are illuminated with the divine possibilities of people being renewed and restored as they gather in the presence of the Lord. This is why we see them coming every week to the house of God.

They keep coming because they claim their position in God's righteousness and refuse to permit the quenching of their faith. As leaders, our role is to encourage and challenge them to realize *shrinking back* is the "unthinkable thought." Lenski said, "The galaxy of the men and women of faith is an inspiring army." As we consider the list of faith heroes in Hebrews, we are exhorted to build an army of champions.

With this thought in mind, year after year, I continue to hammer upon one dynamic drumbeat to set the cadance for the army I am pastoring. My dream is for them to move forward in a sound Biblical-based faith. We mark our progress as a church by this theme we call, "Moving forward!"

Exodus 14:15. (NAS) Then the Lord said to Moses, "Why are you crying out to Me? Tell the sons of Israel to go forward."

Our growth as a church is marked by two statements of faith. Linked directly with this theme are the positive affirmations, *'Yes, I Can . . .Yes, He Can. . .Yes, We Can!'* The banners draped from the ceiling across the front of our church repeat the **YES, I CAN** theme, because I believe what we most frequently see and meditate upon, we become. And, if we are serious about pleasing God and want to know how to live the adventurous and wholesome Christian life, then we need to learn more about this terrific subject called faith.

Faith is substance. . .

> **Hebrews 11:1.** (NAS) Now faith is the assurance of things hoped for, the conviction of things not seen.

During recent times, it seems there has been a greater emphasis upon the teaching of faith than ever before in history. While definitions abound, there is perhaps no more complete and accurate definition of faith and one more generally applicable than what we find in Hebrews.

Faith is . . . "the Title Deed, confidence, substructure, substance of things hoped for." Hebrews 11:1 says,

> **Hebrews 11:1.** (ASV) "Now faith is *assurance* of things hoped for. . ."
> (WEY) "Now faith is a *confident assurance* of that for which we hope. . ."
> (MON) "Now faith is the *Title Deed* of things hoped for. . ."
> (NEB) "What is faith? Faith gives *substance* to our hopes. . ."
> (LENSKI) "There is such a thing as faith, namely a *firm confidence.*"

Substance defined:

A definition of *substance* is, "Reality which gives a firm guarantee" . . .; "underlying reality behind something" . . .; "proof of things one cannot see." These definitions point out that things which have no reality in themselves are *made real*, given the *substance* of faith. Through the thinking eye of faith we see visionary potential in realities that display no material evidence. The reality-substance is no less real because it does not exist in the natural. Faith is active, living and motivating us forward by means of God's resurrection power. It enables us to have confidence to believe the reality-substance actually exists in the unseen. Only *faith* gives us genuine assurance of this certainty! That is why the prayer of a righteous man is heard by God. Like Jesus, He sees what His Father is doing. The prayer of faith believes you have already received the thing that was prayed for.

Mark 11:24. What things soever you desire, when you pray, believe that ye receive them, ye shall have them.

Faith is not believing that God can — but that God will!

Faith is conviction...

Faith *sees* the invisible, believes the incredible and receives the impossible! *Seeing* the invisible is holy conviction welling up inside me like a river. A celebrating church invokes the positive, seeing experience of faith in all who attend. Even hardened hearts are convinced and melt like wax when the presence of the Lord is made visible in joyous worship.

Hebrews 11:27. (NAS) By faith he (Moses) left Egypt, not fearing the wrath of the King; for he endured, as seeing Him who is unseen.

Conviction is an important term if the Christian is to get a firm grip on faith. If we cannot *move* in the Holy Spirit, we cannot understand God or move confidently in the Kingdom of God, for His Kingdom is spiritual, not natural or tangible. When we move in the Spirit of God, we can touch what is invisible and make it visible. A celebrating church is not a mix of weird people displaying strange behavior. No, a cameo of a celebrating church is a body of believers who trust God and move in the power of the Holy Spirit in response to His leading. This is only possible by means of *conviction*.

Conviction — Elenkos — 'A proof or test... may be used as a legal term with a meaning like cross examination. Evidence — the proving of things not seen.'

The paradox of faith is to believe what we do not see, and the reward of this faith is to *see* what we believe because of conviction!

Faith is the bedrock basis of all that we ever will hope for. Faith extends our vision as seen by the eyes of the heart. Faith moves our viewpoint beyond reason, what we learn by our senses. . . for faith, like love, has its *own reasons.*

To believe, but not demonstrate belief is to not believe! Faith, hope and demonstration are inseparable elements of one concept. You cannot have one without the other. An old proverb says "Seeing is believing." The Bible promises, "Believing is seeing." Faith is doing what you believe.

When the human soul so relies upon God that His Word is absolute and sufficient for its certainties, this reliance upon faith has in it the potency of spirit. It is as sure of the promised blessing as if it were a tangible present possession.

Faith is believing. . .

John 20:27-29. (NAS) Then Jesus said to Thomas, "Reach here your finger, and see My hands; and reach here your hand, and put it into My side; and be not unbelieving, but believing."

Thomas answered and said to Him, "My Lord and my God!"

Jesus said to him, "Because you have seen Me, have you believed? Blessed are they who did not see, and yet believed."

Sense knowledge hinders the healthy activity of a living, flourishing faith. Sense knowledge requires *sense-evidence.* "Except I can see. . . I will not believe," were the feelings of doubting Thomas. Sense knowledge trusts in feelings, emotions, hearing, tasting, and smelling. The contrast of Bible faith is 180 degrees opposite. A living faith acts upon the Word independent of any sense evidence. This faith is established only upon God's Word. The cameo of a celebrating church includes teaching God's Word about faith and its effectiveness for daily living.

Abraham's faith. . .

One of God's faith heroes is the father of faith. Abraham

had faith for what he could not see.

Romans 4:17-21. (NAS) As it is written, "A father of many nations have I made you" in the sight of Him whom he believed, even God, who gives life to the dead and calls into being that which does not exist.

In hope against hope he believed, in order that he might become a father of many nations, according to that which had been spoken, "So shall your descendents be."

And without becoming weak in faith he contemplated his own body, now as good as dead since he was about a hundred years old, and the deadness of Sarah's womb;

yet with respect to the promise of God, he did not waver in unbelief, but grew strong in faith, giving glory to God,

and being fully assured that what He had promised, He was able also to perform.

A "trusting God portrait" would feature Abraham as the ideal model.

As we review Romans 4:17-21, we examine the model image of a faith that believes. Our goal is to make faith relevant!

Verse 4:17—God calls into existence the things that do not exist and speaks of future events with as much certainty as though they were already past history. God speaks His word even to those yet unborn.

Q. What word has God spoken to you regarding the visionary plan for your church and yet unborn converts? What future events exist in your heart that will bring forth a celebrating congregation?

Verse 4:18—With no ground for hope, Abraham sustained by hope, put his faith in God.

Q. In 25 words or less, can you define the hope you have in your heart for the people God brings to your church for ministry?

Verse 4:19—Being not weak in faith even when he faced the utter impotence of his own body, which he called "good as dead," he faced the prophetic facts with faith.

Q. Can you name the character defects in your life that are totally unmanageable unless faith attracts God's power to empower you?

Verse 4:20—He did not stagger with unbelief, but by the strength of his faith he claimed the promise and refused to waiver.

Q. What plan of action are you embarking upon and what promises of God are you standing on to improve and expand your corporate gatherings?

Verse 4:20—He gave glory to God, praised God for His blessing and promise before it ever happened.

Q. Are you praising God who gives life to the dead and calls into being that which does not exist? Is your rejoicing congregation celebrating the promises of faith?

Verse 4:21—He was fully convinced and absolutely certain that what God promised, He was able to perform.

The questions presented in the context of Abraham's faith are critical and vital if the influence of leadership is as important as we believe it to be. There are many studies which reveal the personality and spirit of a church mimic the personality and spiritual characteristics of the leadership.

No matter what current or foreseen impossibilities loom before us as part and parcel of the promises involved. . .like making the dead come alive. . .calling the non-existent as existent. . .and no matter what sound reasons call for doubting with unbelief. . .faith remains as the bottom line.

Being fully persuaded means—'To be full of a thing.' Faith says I can have it when I can't see it! And faith says the timeline is NOW. The cameo of a rejoicing church includes a living faith.

Faith is power————

Whoever you are. . .whatever your need. . .the thing we all need more of today is POWER! We find all the power we need in trusting God.

Hebrews 11:2. (AMP) For by faith and trust and holy fervor born of faith, the men of old had divine testimony borne to them and obtained a good report.

Definition of Trust. . .
The dictionary defines trust as, "Confidence, or reliance or resting of the mind on the *integrity*, justice or other sound principle of another person. To place confidence in or rely on."

As I mentioned in the preceding chapter, the kingdom of this world is passing away, but the Kingdom of God is secure and external. The certainty of faith reminds us that when this planet runs its course and passes away, all that will remain will be the Word and the Bride, God's church!

If we are to rely on and put our confidence in anything, we need absolute trust in the integrity of that thing. The same is true in trusting God. Being convicted of the importance of this principle, I was determined to conceptualize the very integrity of God before the eyes of our congregation in the banners, church bulletins, posters, newsletters, and prayer guidelines. And in sermons, I repeatedly remind our church that the integrity of God is:

Fair, Wise, Eternal, Loving, Caring, Holy, Kind, Forgiving, Responsive, Healing, Faithful, Merciful, Accessible, Good, Gracious, Reliable, Sufficient, and the God who is NOW.

Scriptures about trust include: Psalms 5:11, 20:7; 44:6; 49:6; 56:3; 62:8; Proverbs 3:5; 28:25; 29:25; 30:5; II Corinthians 1:9 and I Timothy 4:10.

92

The cameo of a rejoicing church includes a positive and powerful experience in each and every corporate gathering. The vibrant power of the Holy Spirit is released the more we praise and celebrate our absolute trust in the integrity of God.

Faith is confession. . .

Champions in Christ everywhere acknowledge the power of the tongue is like a rudder directing the course of a great ship.

Proverbs 18:21. (NAS) Death and life are in the power of the tongue, and those who love it will eat of its fruit.

Philippians 4:13. (NAS) Nothing is beyond my power in the strength of Him who makes me strong.

I Timothy 1:12. (NAS) And I thank Christ Jesus my Lord who hath made me equal to the task!

The cameo of a rejoicing church tells us that the disciplined Christian life includes a positive confession of God's Word. Speaking faith will shape and fashion your life. To help align the hearts and minds of our body of believers with the Word of God, I have created a *"YES. . .I CAN! CHAMPIONS CREED."* It is published on a durable glossy stock and is available to believers everywhere. Many keep it with their Bible. Storing the *YES, I CAN* promises of God in the heart will cause faith to increase and greater power to flow among those who are committed to live as champions in Jesus Christ.

The Cameo of a Celebrating Church

A cameo is a treasured and beautiful portrait of someone precious. Our final chapter of this book has portrayed numerous brush strokes to unveil this godly cameo of Jesus.

93

A celebrating church is a positive experience when people are ushered into His Presence. . .when a strained faith is strengthened . . .a defeated faith is perfected and a strong faith is firmed up. The Presence of God can be felt when we enter into His Presence. The believer is inspired, strengthened and empowered to overcome and live for others as servants of the Most High. And when we attract the backsliders, the unsaved, and other Christians searching for a church home to settle into. . . it is the felt-presence of Jesus that touches lives and makes corporate gatherings powerful. As this book was being completed, a spontaneous prayer was given by the author as he opened a corporate gathering worship service. It was recorded and included as a fitting way to end this book. It is a prayer for you every time you gather with God's people and are ushered into his felt-presence.

PRAYER:

In the name of Jesus, we come to the very throne of God. We ask that there would be a release right now of that oil, the symbol of the Holy Spirit. Lord, we know that you have fresh oil for every believer. Lord, your oil is always fresh in power, able to meet every need, able to supply whatever we have need of. Lord, right now just strengthen every believer's heart — the minds, the spirit. Father, let Jesus just flow in this service right now, in the name of Jesus. Lord, just flow from one believer to another. Lord, just let the life of God begin to flow one to another. Lord, just release the very life of the anointing of Jesus in our midst. Lord, bring healing right now to those who need to be healed in their bodies. Lord, bring healing to those who need to be healed of their emotions, their inner person, Lord, their minds. Lord, bring a word of encouragement, bring a word of faith to every person in the name of the Lord Jesus Christ. Lord, we believe that you can heal that marriage which is lacking. Lord, you can heal that young person who is thinking about drugs or alcohol or doing that which is immoral. Lord, you can minister to every person right where we live. Lord, we offer ourselves to you right now; we lift up our hearts, our minds to you, Lord. Cleanse us in the name of Jesus from a Babylonian society. Lord, a society that would rob us of godly values. Lord, the values of your kingdom, the values of honesty and integrity. The values of purity. Lord, cleanse us right now. Let us be a people set apart, not in some weird way, but in a very real way — set apart unto you, in the name of Jesus.

Amen

Conclusion

As we practice the principles outlined in this book, we find that worship services *can* become the dynamic explosion of God's presence that they were meant to be. Let us not give in to the pressure of "abandoning the assembling together" as so many leaders are doing. Corporate gatherings are a major source of strength for those in our flock, which includes families, businessmen, college students, single parents, young people, and women. We *all* need His presence to overcome the many pressures of today's world. The presence of God can change our lives, attitudes, and characters when nothing else can successfully penetrate these areas.

If we will sincerely teach and pray these principles into existence, then we will experience the power God ordained for our corporate gatherings. As a prayer and a challenge to each leader, let us conclude by meditating on the beautiful expression of God's power released in a righteous corporate body found in Psalm 133 (AMP):

Psalm 133. (AMP) Behold, how good and how pleasant it is for brethren to dwell together in unity!

It is like the precious ointment poured on the head, that ran down on the beard, even the beard of Aaron [the first high priest], that came down upon the collar and skirts of his garments [consecrating his whole body];

Like the dew of [lofty] Mount Hermon, and the dew that comes on the hills of Zion; for there the Lord has commanded the blessing, even life forevermore [upon the high and lowly].

As leaders who are convinced of this truth, let us endeavor to intercede and see the Lord bring Psalm 133 into our congregations — the anointing that runs down from the *Head* to the *whole body*.

Question: Can I be a Christian without attending the church?

Answer: Yes, it is possible. It is something like being:

A student who will not go to school.

A soldier who will not join an army.

A citizen who does not pay taxes or vote.

A salesman with no customers.

An explorer with no base camp.

A seaman on a ship without a crew.

A businessman on a deserted island.

An author without readers.

A tuba player without an orchestra.

A parent without a family.

A football player without a team.

A politician who is a hermit.

A scientist who does not share his findings.

A bee without a hive.

—*Wesleyan Christian Advocate*

Notes

[1]Paul Kurtz, ed., *Humanist Manifestos I and II*. Buffalo: Prometheus Books, 1982, p. 10.

[2]Ibid., p. 13.

Bibliography

Green, Wigram. *The New Englishman's Greek Concordance and Lexicon*. Laffayette, IN: Jay P. Green, 1982.

Kittel, Gerhard and Friedrich, Gerhard. *Theological Dictionary of the New Testament*. Grand Rapids: Wm. B. Eerdmans Publishing Company, 1976.

Strong, James. *Strong's Exhaustive Concordance*. Grand Rapids: Baker Book House, 1983.

Thayer, Joseph Henry. *A Greek-English Lexicon of the New Testament*. Wilmington, DE: Jay P. Green, 1977.

Vine, W.E. *Vine's Expository Dictionary of Old and New Testament Words*, ed. F. F. Bruce. Old Tappan, NJ: Flemming H. Revell, 1981.

Webster's Dictionary, Ninth New Collegiate. Springfield, MA: Merriam-Webster, Inc., 1984.